T0198531

Titles by *Langaa*

The Lord

of Anomy

Basil Diki

Langaa Research & Publishing CIG
Mankon, Bamenda

Publisher:
Langaa RPCIG
(*Langaa* Research & Publishing Common Initiative Group)
P.O. Box 902 Mankon
Bamenda
North West Region
Cameroon
Langaagrp@gmail.com
www.langaa-rpcig.net

Distributed outside N. America by African Books Collective
orders@africanbookscollective.com
www.africanbookscollective.com

Distributed in N. America by Michigan State University
Press
msupress@msu.edu
www.msupress.msu.edu

ISBN: 9956-558-67-2

DISCLAIMER

This is a work of fiction. Names, characters, places, and incidents are either the author's invention or they are used fictitiously. Any resemblance to actual places and persons, living or dead, events, or locales is coincidental.

Contents

Act IV

Introduction

The play is a work of art put together with distinct craftsmanship clearly for entertainment and academic reasons. It exploits allegory, conundrums and various tools to depict with great skill and reproduce in the mind of the reader / audience the pictures and atmosphere reminiscent of 1875 Southern Africa, her tribes and the mentality of foreigners to that land. Of particular interest and uniqueness to the work is the missionary astonished to learn that he has come to a people almost conversant with Christianity and Islam, the natives having distinctly learnt these from the Portuguese and Arabic traders decades ahead of his advent.

Basil Diki's scant and expert use of poetry, eclogue and juxtaposition of contradictory elements is masterly. The play's level of debate is highly judicial and academic. The story itself provokes debate, both academic and religious, while enhancing judgmental skills. It's designed to improve the reader's / audience's command of both written and spoken English, oratory skills and the benevolent use of coercion and coaxing. The play offers ethnographic elements with regards the Rozvi of present day Zimbabwe and the Zulu of South Africa.

It offers insight into African religious beliefs and convictions and is of profound relevance to African studies. The overall objective is to produce an analytical and highly conversant literature in English for the scholar, teacher or lecturer. What struck me the most is the high level of technicality and the ease with which the playwright expresses himself in English, the unpredictability of the story, the never-ending climaxes, the suspense in literally every scene and the haunting ending.

To compare the playwright to any modern dramatist is to demean him. The quality of such writing is reflective of a genius at work in a domain of his comfort and in which he has invested many years. It doesn't surprise me that Basil Diki has won awards before for his literal and theatrical achievements. The manner he develops and handles conflicts provides classic study in itself of plots and subplots, comprehension of character and motive, and offers insight into the unpredictability of the human mind in a crisis. The only seeming frailty I found was that I desired to 'see' more of the sly Sir Wilkie Crowler whom I had longed to encounter from the suspense of the expository scenes. But, however, had he appeared in more scenes *The Lord of Anomy* would have been too voluminous to stage.

This is undoubtedly great scholarly work for the student, lecturer and professor of Literature in English / Literal studies and Humanities. In my humble opinion *The Lord of Anomy* is a brilliant, unforgettable and gripping classic masterpiece. This work is set to grab awards in literal circles at international level. Congratulations, Africa!

Dr. W. Mupamombe Chuma
Harare, 2009

Characters

Changamire Zunzanyika	Rozvi King
Dombo	King's younger brother
Gungwa	King's son, adolescent
Chikukwa	King's Aide
Chemusango	Hermit, dread-logged
Sekuru Rondangozi	Regal spirit medium
Gagi	Rondangozi's acolyte
Mmabatho	An impi warrior, ferocious giant
Drao Ferenado	A porter

Chapwanya
Chinake
Gundu
Kapingu   } Elders
Makeredza
Nyamaropa

Rev. Abraham Holbrook	British Missionary
Shannon Forrester	Holbrook's Aide & Chronicler
Sir Wilkie Crowler	British Politician

Plus: A drummer, a muscular swordsman, 6 elders, 7 porters &
    12 warriors.

Act I

Scene 1

1ˢᵗ Day. Afternoon. King Zunzanyika's courtyard.

(Attended, the king is seated on a rustic wooden throne in the background. Wrapped in expensive imported cloth and spotting a pair of sandals he is be-jewelled with a distinctive sapphire around his neck and amulets and charms around his wrists and ankles. His headgear of ostrich feathers and porcupine spikes lends an ethnic distinction. The scene is dreary; the king sits under a grass-thatched shade facing an unpaved open space surrounded by circular primitive huts of poles and clay.

Chikukwa, the regal aide, stands to his master's immediate right. A bodyguard of eight warriors in loincloths, two bearing long-barrelled assault guns, the rest arrows and spears, stand behind the king and his aide. To the left and detached is a Drummer with a drum strapped around his neck. Seated to the king's right on low wooden benches and stools, and perpendicular to him, is a cluster of twelve elders including Chapwanya, Chinake, Gundu, Kapingu, Makeredza and Nyamaropa. The elders are sharing snuff, sniffing it and conversing quietly. On a reed mat on the ground before the elders are spirit-medium Rondangozi and his acolyte, Gagi. Rondangozi is heavily beaded and sits with legs spread before him while his torso is entirely covered in a black and white cloth, a combination of two equal fabrics sewn together. The medium groans and grunts, and occasionally shakes his head stoically. Gagi sits at ease beside him, his knees propped up. On the same mat are a beaded gourd, a wand from an animal tail and two corked cattle horns.

King Zunzanyika nods at Chikukwa who waves at the Drummer who beats the drum thrice, bringing silence forthwith, except for the noises made by the medium.)

Chikukwa

(Addressing the elders)

Elders, it pleases the king to salute you for your courage in assisting him face a faceless menace in these extraordinarily apprehensive times. These are times of uncertainty and terror, and strangely, of seemingly authentic ancestral voices unnerving their own. Neither in living memory nor in ancestral legends are soothsayers, sorcerers and augurs known to have fled the land. Their flight is a phenomenal disgrace, so asserts Changamire Zunzanyika. He deplores it with the vilest epithets.

The elders nod and clap their hands in agreement.

Most families have taken a cue from the diviners and fled into the wilderness, adjudging predators to be a lesser threat than the visitors in our custody. At this court we've received all manner of foreign visitors; ranging from haters of the foreskin in skullcaps, to cattle worshippers with scarlet dots on their brows. Yet, we were never relentlessly forewarned against them. The Rozvi were naturally thrifty with their foreskins. Consecrated bulls, yes, we worship, but we saw bowing to the generality of cattle as utterly beneath us. These propagators of foreign divinities just left us quietly like a mist. Today the Council of Elders is augustly called upon to assist the throne make a progressive decision. In a predatory realm, the prey is often captivated by the fangs of its destroyer. From our enemy, the cockroach brought to us by merchants, let us learn to probe, which indeed is the reason for this gathering. But the king prays your indefatigable caution for a sound resolution that causes no undue alarm.

Makeredza raises a hand, Chikukwa gestures at him to rise. He rises.

Makeredza
(Hands clasped in humility and bowing slightly)

Changamire, I adore you. Elders, I salute you. Our diviners said the sojourning wayfarer was a prophetic figure, meaning a prophet was sent to us. Can we execute a god-sent emissary and feel no remorse about it? I thank you.e

Makeredza sits, some elders nod in concurrence.

Chikukwa
Changamire notes your concern and will duly address it.

Chapwanya raises a hand. Chikukwa gestures at him to rise.

Chapwanya
(Rises. Bowing, head tilted in humility)

My salutations to the king and the elders. Our diviners spoke of a coming condemning voice. That voice has come as prophesied and is in our midst, and our seers have fled –the fifteen of them. For years they guarded our thoughts and decisions, and to their voice we harkened religiously. Now it's apparent we were being led by cowardly crabs, ferocious-looking, but quick to scramble for cover upon the slightest threat. I feel betrayed, but take solace in the fact that cowardice is synonymous with mutiny and punishable by death. I thank you. *(Sits)*

5

Chikukwa

The king hears you well, Chapwanya. The fate of the diviners he'll declare to us, for this is something that also irks him most terribly.

Kapingu

I have questions. (*Rises*) Has divination, our own lifeblood, foredoomed us? Could this be a divine conspiracy to destabilize the kingdom? Is it a case of misinterpretation of bones? Did our augurs misinterpret the cries of the ugly salamander? Should we too take flight into the hills and mountains? Must we embark on the route to exile? (*Pauses*) Ignorance darkens counsel, and death is a stealthy untimely stalker. Should the Council be limited in its resolutions, then this meeting is just a fallacious gathering of elders and their king, I regret to say. After calamitous consequences, I foresee the Council being called upon to gather again. Then it shall be reminiscent of a committee of vultures, which only meets after the occurrence of death. I thank you. (*Sits*)

Chikukwa

But presently the pertinent issue is the menace. (*Pause*) If no one will voice his mind may it please Changamire Zunzanyika to address the Council, after which the wayfarers shall be arraigned?

Zunznyika

I greet you and welcome you to this court. Of cockroaches, my aide spoke, and I applaud him. We're not here to build Noah's Ark to cower in like cockroaches. Nor are we here to admire a grotto. For the first time, we're partially on our own and must think or the predicament will consume us as we bicker about the cowardice of our seers. Due credit goes to Sekuru Rondangozi and his acolyte. He didn't flee in the face of the so-called impending disaster, and will assist us in demystifying this enigma. But his word shall be crippled because no other diviners will confirm it. (*Emphatic pause*) The whole thing could be nothing but an octopus way out of the sea in search of tender prey. Or at the end, we might learn that the alarm was nothing but the eventless singing of a cicada. All that noise from rubbing its legs against its wings doesn't amount to a threat. The seers urged us not to kill them, or devastation would befall us. But if we so decide, we'll terminate the aliens. The diviners, too, if the Council so decides. (*Pause*) Let an honest assessment govern us, not premeditated brutality, or we might end up slaughtering the man who brings us rain. The sojourners will be brought from the pit now.

Chikukwa

Arraignment! Sekuru Rondangozi to preside!

(Chikukwa waves at the Drummer, who strikes the drum momentarily. Enter Rev. Abraham Holbrook and Shannon Forrester escorted by three spear-wielding warriors. The elders murmur resentment and surprise at the appearance of the missionaries. The two stand forlornly before the elders and the king, the warriors behind them. They're in 19th century attire; the Reverend is in a high-waisted and sleeved waistcoat, baggy shirt and trousers, and Shannon is in a hopped long skirt and a frilly lace blouse. Both are dishevelled and soiled. Rondangozi rises, picking up a corked horn, which he uncorks and pours an ash-like powder onto his right palm, all the while eyeing the missionaries. Gagi rises, too, with the gourd and the animal tail. The medium gingerly steps towards the missionaries his right hand poised to cast the powder. Two paces shy of the missionaries he stops and appraises them, the hand still poised his countenance an intimidating mask. The Reverend remains calm but Shannon cowers behind him. The medium smiles, lets out an angry growl then casts the powder on the two, briefly blanketing them in an ashy plume. The missionaries cough, sneeze and recoil but the warriors behind shove them forward. Rondangozi drops the horn, snatches the tail from his acolyte, quickly dips it in the gourd and begins to sprinkle the two with water, which one gathers is repugnant from the expressions on their faces and their feeble attempts to cover their noses with their hands. He continues to dip the wand and sprinkle them until both stoop haplessly, and, almost drenched, retch dryly. The medium and his acolyte return to the mat and sit as before, Rondangozi waving the wand.)

Here they are, elders, for your appraisal. They walked through the city gates yesterday afternoon in the company of eight porters from Sofala. Word of their arrival quickly spread. All the eight villages were soon restless with fear. The exodus into the hills and mountains began. Meanwhile, warriors immediately arrested the trespassers, the whole lot and their baggage.

Chinake

If the rest were porters, fellow ethnic men from Sofala, then we must be ashamed of ourselves. How can this man and woman before us, both unarmed and hapless, shake Ibwe and send clansmen scurrying for safety into the wilderness?

7

Kapingu

I'm told the two refused violently to be turned away; they preferred death instead. Death should've been given them to satisfy their death-wish. Our Spirit-elders have always protected us. Was it foretold that ancestral spirits would desert us, too?

Gundu

The diviners lied and are guilty of perjury. This day is an awful disappointment! I had hoped Sekuru Rondangozi would make a public spectacle of the trespassers.

Kapingu

Had a battle-axe been handy I'd have beheaded them and brought an end to the indecision we are now made to suffer. In battle indecision can cost lives, but here nobody knows whether we're at war or not.

Nyamaropa

If we interview them they'll tell us what the haters of the foreskins told us: that they've brought us the greatest of gifts and have no interests in matters of the state. If we kill them this Council shall forever be blamed for every mishap that might befall the Rozvi.

Gundu

In future, whether predicted or not, such wanderers deserve summary executions for the stability of Urozviland. This meeting would've been avoided.

Makeredza

Causing undue panic isn't my province. But, as a precautionary measure, I must prod you to regard the white-skins as perilous until we learn otherwise. From the death-feigning puff-adder let us take our lesson. Ordinarily it appears harmless, yet it is one of the most venomous vipers. If I sound self-contradictory it is because I've taken the path of sound judgment.

Chinake

Makeredza puts it very well, elders. I'm not for the erection of a monument to fear, but say this after due consideration; give heed to the utterances of the soothsayers and the sorcerers for they couldn't all have spoken vainly unless they had reason to lie to us, which hitherto is unfounded. We run the risk of turning this meeting into an inauguration of a season of anomy if we completely disregard the diviners' warning.

Chapwanya

Let them speak or we are here to gawk at white-skins.

Chikukwa

Elders have no reason to marvel at foreigners having grown tired of seeing them come and go as merchants and religious figures. Speak they will. Changamire concurs. But be careful; nobody understands the extent of the power of coercion on their tongues. The tongues of Hindu traders disarm cobras. The serpents end up dancing to flute music against their will. The charmers' cramped baskets become the homes of these once vicious snakes. Take cognizance of this. (*To the king*) If it pleases Changamire, the elders wish to interview the arrivals.

Zunzanyika

All the allusions were serpentine; none reminded us of the peaceful dove. Of your resentment, suspicions, intolerance and the need for caution you spoke. But stress I this to the Council: Indeed we're not here to marvel at foreigners as if they're metamorphic, long lost relatives finally back to claim kin. These travellers could be from Cairo, Baghdad or Tunis – great ancient cities of grandeur. They could be from the much talked about Vatican and bear Peter's bones as a charm to blind us. But that shouldn't confuse our priorities. Their eyes are looking at idolaters and sodomites. When we open our mouths their ears hear paganism spoken in the original voice of the Devil. The utterances of such people are predictable; therefore we shouldn't be in a hurry to interview them. Do I speak in Arabic parables, Chikukwa?

Chikukwa

Sir, we hear you, Changamire.
(*Bowing slightly at him*)

Zunzanyika

Of immediate concern to me are my subjects cowering needlessly in the wilderness, perhaps alongside pythons or in the territory of leopards. Some may have been devoured by now. For these refugees my heart grieves. I order that SDrummers be sent to every hill, to every mountain, to every forest, and summon clansmen back to their homes. Against fear I've always spoken to clansmen, beseeching them fatherly. Now, I'm taking up arms against chicken-heartedness, a liability no kingdom needs. (*Rises*) This is the

9

ultimatum to be made plain to the dastard: Return before noon tomorrow or you effectively banish yourself from Urozviland. By noon tomorrow the hangman should've set up the scaffold in the marketplace. Regiments are to comb the remnant cowards from every thicket, kopje and cave, and commandeer them to the executioner. This goes for the diviners too, should they be sighted, the fifteen of them. Spare children and suckling mothers. (*Briefly stares at the missionaries*) Tomorrow, as the four trap-doors of the scaffold open and close, we seal the fate of the aliens.

Chikukwa

This meeting stands adjourned till the same time tomorrow. Cast them in the pit!

As the three warriors impersonally grab the missionaries and drag them away, exit King Zunzanyika attended. Some elders nod, some shake their heads, and some gape in shock, but Chapwanya claps his hands in appreciation.

Curtain.

Scene 2

2ⁿᵈ Day. Afternoon.

(Scene same as Scene One. Except for the bodyguard, the warriors and the missionaries, the characters have had a change of clothes. The missionaries are already arraigned, but seated on low stools directly facing the Council of Elders. Shannon is scribbling on a jotter using a feather which she is constantly dipping in an ink bottle at her feet. Chikukwa is stooped, taking instructions from King Zunzanyika. After a while he straightens up and faces the elders.)

Chikukwa

Yesterday all of us were ready to avert a crisis, which turned out to be nothing more than a freak mediumistic hoax. Yesterday the hills and mountains rang with drumbeats and broadcasts. Yesterday most clansmen and their families were prevailed upon to return to their homesteads. *(Pause)* Today, those of you who passed through the marketplace saw the scaffold and the hangman awaiting his preys. A crowd was already gathering around the towering scaffold.

Chapwanya and a few elders nod eagerly.

But, bad luck seems to dog that scaffold; the regiments have not left for the forests, due to a stubborn refusal by General Gwenhere and the military helm. The commanders argued moralistically against forcibly subduing fellow clansmen. Gwenhere made it clear that if Changamire insists the General will have to resign. The fact of the matter is that his family is still in hiding. So are his in-laws.

Gundu

Mutiny is only punishable by death and never atoned by resignation.

Chikukwa

Changamire will make a public spectacle of the General and his commanders tomorrow. The scaffold shall not be dismantled. It is definitely assured action tomorrow!

Chapwanya

(Nodding and smiling)

This fight against cowardice and mutiny, if genuine, persuades me we're on the path out of a premature, menopausal stalemate. The old, expansive Urozviland of Dombolakochingwano, our founder, is about to be reborn. May it be the will of the spirits that Changamire lives forever!

11

Elders
(Gutturally in unison)
May the spirits grant him a long life!

Chapwanya
Let nothing stay the executions. Could the white-skins have brought us blessings after all?

Chikukwa
It is too early, Chapwanya, for speculative conclusions. Today we will hear them and weigh their words against what was divined. As we do, let us ceaselessly ask ourselves if we're so decadent and heinous that foreign gods should send us a deistic emissary. In all the cardinal points, rape, incest and mutilations are rampant and thriving, all of them worse than the debauched Sodom and the Gomorrah the traders from the far north preached about.

Rondangozi
(Baffled. Points at Shannon)
She has been at it for a long time now. What is she doing?
Chikukwa sharply beckons Rev. Holbrook to rise. He does.

Chikukwa
(Solemnly)
It pleases our king, addressed in humility as *Changamire*, and the honourable elders of Ibwe City, to hear you exonerate yourself. Let not the woman beside you sway you from your defence. Opt for machismo but beware, death awaits.

Holbrook
(Humbly clapping his hands)
Changamire, I greet and submit myself to you. Elders, I greet and humble myself before you. *(Stops clapping)* I am Rev. Abraham Holbrook, a Christian missionary from the Evangelical Church of England. *(Stoops slightly and taps Shannon on the shoulder)* This here is Shannon Forrester, my aide and chronicler, but basically a fellow Christian.
Shannon briefly stops scribbling, waves and smiles at the elders, but everyone simply stares back at her. She in turn stares back at them then reverts to scribbling.

Rondangozi
(To Rev. Holbrook clearly having lost his temper)
I asked a question, stranger. She has been ... *(mimes scribbling)*... for some time now. What is she doing?

12

Holbrook

Sir, she is recording the proceedings. Like I said, she is my chronicler, one who compiles a clinical record of my daily activities and important meetings like the one underway.

Rondangozi

I can't see why you suppose such a record is essential. She is still young and productive. She shouldn't have journeyed to this land of bats and vultures to perish most ruthlessly. She should have remained in your homeland and given herself to meaningful work, like winnowing grain and grinding. Why do you abuse her so? Why do you bring a poor woman to her death in an unyielding wilderness?

Holbrook

It is her heartfelt calling to be a servant of the High God in the remotest of lands. (*Smiling and calm*) Rejoice for this is your season. The Supreme Being, not the god of rain, not the god of fruitfulness, or the god of the rivers, has sent us to your land to reclaim a desolate heritage. Today you ought to celebrate, not sharpen machetes nor erect a scaffold.

Chikukwa

So far you've said nothing in your defence. Changamire isn't interested in rhetoric. The belittling of our gods offends him. Stranger, be warned! *Your* life is at stake!

Holbrook

We bring you the gospel. Neither self-interest nor sense-gratification governs us. We don't have the remotest intention to enrich ourselves. State affairs are out of bounds to us and we promise not to delve into them. We submit ourselves to all your laws, customs and tenets that are not offensive to the High God. (*Looking at the king*) Sir, I found your knowledge of cities including the Vatican impressive, and take it you have a working understanding of Christianity, which would make my discourses with you easier.

Chikukwa

From lips Arabic, Castilian and Portuguese, Changamire had the good fortune to learn about the world and the bible. But these teachers of his weren't preceded by unnerving prophecies or the flight of diviners.

Makeredza

Though clansmen rejected the teachings of the Gurus, the Imams and the Sheiks, they didn't despise Allah or any foreign gods. And the foreigners didn't blaspheme our spirit-elders.

Holbrook

I apologise if I have unwittingly offended. I meant none. But know from the onset that I didn't travel this far to offer you aromatic praise poetry. Neither did I come to cringe in fear at the sight of some figure. To man I'll render due respect, but to God alone will/shall I bow. Pleading for my life is outside my faith.

Chinake

Oh! You came to sow Christianity in a rocky field of cacti. Take this immaculate gospel elsewhere. Our neighbours are ever too eager to please aliens.

Holbrook

Thank you, elder, for the advice, but this land of yours is our destination. We set out to come to Urozviland. Since our arrival we have taken time to learn Rozvi. This is our destination.

Kapingu

Frankly, you came expecting to meet ape-men in utter darkness. Now that supposed baboons can give you a Mohammedan and a biblical tutelage would you insist on staying?

Holbrook

Pity you heard *about* the gospel from the wrong mouths. Mouths that solicited your acceptance of dubious religions couldn't have earnestly taught you about salvation. (*Spreading his arms*) I didn't come to prattle *about* the gospel. I come to you in the name of God!

Rondangozi

The high God you speak of. What authority do you have to speak in the name of this fearsome God?

Holbrook

I'm not earthly. I represent the high God....

Rondangozi

(*Interjects*)

Don't just ejaculate, stranger, the gods are listening. The high God you talk about is too far-fetched and remote to be concerned with man. His chief concerns are the seasons. Man is too minute for him.

Holbrook
(*Smiling*)
Sir, that's the darkness I came to dispel.

Chikukwa
(*Raises a hand to stop Rev. Holbrook. To the king and briefly to the elders*)
He came to demonstrate machismo.

Zunzanyika
(*Piteously*)
Holbrook, you said your name was. You ought to see our daredevils. They wade into swamps and kill crocodiles with their bare hands, most of them falling prey to the reptiles. If you think that's nothing, visit the *Mosi-wa-Tunya*. As the Zambezi River falls into the great gorge to the roaring pool in the gap's dark depths, you'll find Rozvi clansmen diving along with it. Many plunge into the misty gorge to prove their manliness, but very few emerge. That's machismo, Reverend. It doesn't consist in rhetoric. Arrogantly, you abuse the only chance you have to exonerate yourself. This high God you hold out like a carrot to a donkey has never appealed to anyone in this part of the world.

King Zunzanyika nods at Chikukwa who faces the SDrummer and mimics a sword-like gesture. The SDrummer continually strikes a sombre matching beat. Enter quickly from the background a man in nothing but a red loincloth, carrying a short but thick log on his shoulders. He sets the log in the centre of the courtyard and then exits. Enter from the same point a deliberately slow muscular man whose head is totally covered in a small jute bag with tiny holes for eyes. A cord secures the bag around his neck. The man is in a red loincloth and carries a long sword. Charms and amulets ring his neck and upper arms. He halts at the log, rests the sword's blade on its side against his shoulder, thus, stands statue-like. The drumbeat dies gradually. The missionaries stare intently at the swordsman, as do the elders. Shannon drops the writing materials, rises fearfully and cowers behind the reverend, clinging to his shirt with one hand.

Chikukwa
Changamire, in his endless wisdom, anticipated work to overwhelm the hangman. In an orderly state the timeous execution of justice is an august priority. The swordsman before you is at your disposal should death be your sentence. Then forever the issue of the aliens would rest and our lives would be normal again. (*To the missionaries*)

Fear not. The swordsman is an experienced man of immense corpulence. Since the flight of the diviners a week ago, he has been tirelessly practising on sheep and goats. The sword will have its maiden taste of human blood today, if the sentence so decrees. I assure you, you'll suffer no pain. (*To the elders*) After the executions, Changamire would be glad to hear your honest comments about this new method.

Zunzanyika

While the elders ponder, some semblance of entertainment might be in order. (*To the medium*) Sekuru Rondangozi, kindly show these strangers the strength of our shrines.

Rising, Rondangozi jerks and lets out a startling shriek. Gagi rises, too, bearing the two horns. The medium's voice undulating in an incoherent croon between singing and babbling; without articulate word formation, which he frequently breaks with full body jerks and shrieks. Gagi hands him a horn and returns to pick the gourd on the reed mat, while his master points at Rev. Holbrook with the horn, his actions and sounds becoming wilder and wilder. Gagi sets the gourd between the medium and the missionaries, and retreats to the cluster of elders. The Reverend is calm while his chronicler is beside herself with fright. Suddenly an off-stage scream and a booming yelling voice catches everyone's attention.

Voice
(*Off-stage, booming and panicky*)

Chemusango!... Chemusango!... Chemusango is here!... Chemusango is coming!... Hey!... The comet-man!...

The elders and the king exchange glances and rise in panic. Rondangozi freezes momentarily. Everyone strains to look off-stage in the direction of the growing alarm. The man who brought in the log sprints across the courtyard, so do two women and another man in quick succession. Screams and noises of pandemonium come from off-stage. Exit the elders hastily in the opposite direction. Chikukwa frantically gestures to the three warriors to drag the missionaries away. Exit the missionaries and the three warriors. Everyone fearfully edges towards the farthest corner, but Chikukwa and four of the bodyguard warriors finally break and run, exiting in the same direction as the others.

Enter Chemusango. Exit Gagi, the Drummer and the swordsman panic-stricken. The hermit is tall and deathly collected. He is barefoot, dread-locked and wrapped in black cloth. Two corked slender gourds, calabashes, hang on his sides like handbags i.e. strapped to him like sashes. He stops at the periphery of the courtyard. Everyone stares at him haplessly except for Rondangozi trying to psyche the hermit with a defiant gaze. One after the other the king's remaining bodyguard of four warriors lays down their weapons and prostrates in humility. The king and the medium are left standing.

Chemusango
(Voice cavernous)

Your lamentations summoned me. A season of anomy you dread. In the hermitage I heard your voices and saw the arrivals. Deuced, that's how you feel, and abandoned. Two paths stretch in front of the Rozvi; one leads to ruination, the other to blessings. Only the counsel of a territorial medium can suffice. But, alas, you bank your future on the word of a charlatan, a *n'anga* masquerading as a lion spirit. Continue to consult him to the detriment of the kingdom.

Rondangozi

To what avail do you seek a showdown, Chemusango? Not that you can terrorise me. Clearly, it is of no benefit for mediums to quarrel while our heritage burns. Present your counsel, if you have any.

Chemusango

Changamire, if you knew better you'd banish the charlatan and keep the arrivals. Take heed; remember that when I speak to you I do so as a directive from the spirits. This is their counsel.

Rondangozi
(Breaking from the group)

Nothing worthwhile has ever issued from your mouth, even your appearance forbodes evil. *(Stops two paces from the hermit)*

Chemusango

The Mountain has spoken. The forests beckon me. Offer your respect, minor spirit, and I'll take my leave peacefully.

Rondangozi shakes his head

I offer you peace and you prevaricate. Why are you bent on rousing a holy man? *(Angrily)* Lie down, *n'anga*! Be warned! Your rudeness can yield dire consequences! *(Abruptly calm and dramatically solicitous)* Now, I beseech you; Prostrate in obeisance, Rondangozi, the hermit must take his leave.

Rondangozi

Clansmen might be scared of your evil prowess, but you don't intimidate me. What a pity you thrive on terrorising your own clansmen. In your heart that is synonymous with spiritual supremacy.

Chemusango

A spirit cannot have a heart. I've not come to argue.

Rondangozi

Two territorial mediums cannot co-exist in one kingdom.

Chemusango

A constructive observation, I must say. For that reason one of us must submit or die most terribly.

Rondangozi

(*Pointing at him with the horn*)
Kill me then as proof that you're the authentic one. Kill me with all the savageness you can garner.

Chemusango slowly crosses from the background to the foreground and leaves Rondangozi briefly pointing at nothing before he finally lowers the horn and throws it away. He stops, facing away from everyone.

Chemusango

The hermit doesn't kill clansmen. I'll tell it to the destroyer of life in my hermitage. After his visit you'll know that death is a spirit, not a hermit.

Zunzanyika

I can't stand the two of you demeaning each other in my presence. I order you to stop it. Rather combine your forces now that we're in a crisis for the benefit of the state.

The hermit turns and faces them. He walks towards the king but Rondangozi intercepts him midway. Transfixed, the two exchange stares.

Chemusango

(*To the king, over Rondangozi*)
A donkey and a camel cannot be yoked together. My counsel you already have, Changamire. But expound I this to you as the *n'anga* considers prostrating himself: Existence is a river. A river is a serpent that snakes its course on the riverbed. Because it is a serpent it changes its course ceaselessly. Not all snakes are venomous. The python is a favourite of the spirit-elders.

Zunzanyika
I doubt if I understand you completely.

Chemusango
(*Turns. Walks away from Rondangozi*)
Times are changing. The days of old are over. Our course must change. Look at the white-skins as the favoured pythons. The barren womb shall bear children. Cattle shall multiply. Trees shall sag with fruit. The ears of the urchin shall pop open. Spare the pythons.

As the hermit wanders about, Rondangozi scans the sky and the ground, looking bewildered. He shakes his head. The hermit stops again in the foreground, his hands on the mouths of the calabashes, his back to everyone.

Rondangozi
I peered into the abode of your spirit-elders. Faceless and taciturn they sit, only remotely familiar. From them I could draw no confirmation of your prophecy. I looked yonder. But neither in the clouds, nor on the twenty-eight tabernacles of the moon, nor in the molten depths of the earth, did I see the confirmation I required. Instead I saw vultures and assegais in the fire, and heard a foreign dialect calling clansmen to exile.

The hermit turns and darts across to Rondangozi, confrontationally.

Chemusango
What would a bat see but darkness? Sniff too much of my atmosphere and catch your death, I warn you. (*Steps back as if to go*) Now, prostrate yourself in adoration; I might reward you with a spiritual gift.

Rondangozi
Just where do you get the illusion that I'm your inferior?

Chemusango
Your province is small ailments and cleansing families of misfortune. And you were aptly named: *Ro-nda-ngo-zi* – he who traces vengeful spirits. A man of your limitation isn't supposed to advise a king spiritually. (*Boastfully, and gesticulating wildly*) I prevail on this land, on clansmen and the throne. I preside on all the spirits. I *am* the territorial medium.

Rondangozi
Your presence anywhere is awry. I'd rather die than be bullied. You are only one man, a solitary apparition, who without any logical backup

snuffles in stately affairs. Open your eyes to your nightmarish disposition and your pathetic ministry with neither protégée nor followers. Could a feral livelihood have demented you?

Chemusango
(Sighs)

How brazen! A vulnerable mongoose speaking veritably like a spiritual mogul! (*To the king, over Rondangozi*) Instead of performing his obeisance he blasphemes against the hills and mountains. This he does in your presence, which makes Changamire a witness. What should be his punishment?

Zunzanyika

I'm afraid he voices my concerns, too. (*Voice cracking slightly*) Seven years ago clansmen saw you for the very first time upon your emergence from the wilderness. Your overbearing nature subdued all mediums, and you went on to install me as king. Soon after, you left for the wilderness, only to re-emerge four years later. This is your third appearance.

Chemusango

Would you have preferred a minor spirit to coronate you?

Zunzanyika

I'm not coached in differentiating spirits. What gives me sleepless nights is that your emergence brings with it massive deaths in the villages. Livestock and clansmen, mostly children, succumb. (*Pause*) Your parentage is utterly unknown.

Rondangozi

Neither in Ibwe nor in the entire Urozviland does anyone seem to know you.

Zunzanyika

Who is Chemusango?

Chemusango

Seven years ago I cast snuff on the ground and prayed for your longevity. I petitioned the spirit-elders to enamel you with wisdom. When I was doing all these things why didn't you ask me who I was?

Zunzanyika

I supposed you'd demystify yourself; indeed that was everyone's supposition. But unceremoniously you left and death descended on the eight villages of Ibwe.

Chemusango

(*Turns away again, but remains rooted*)

I see you accuse me of not just witchcraft but atrocities. In your accusations you don't allege but speak firmly with conviction. Can't it wait for the return of the diviners, Changamire?

Zunzanyika

But in the meantime I pray that you go away. Roam the forests as you please but don't set foot in the villages until you learn of the return of the diviners. (*Sternly*) I'm effectively banishing you!

Chemusango

I hear you well, Changamire Zunzanyika. Barking it is undignified for a king. (*Turns and looks at him over Rondangozi*) Knowledge of Asia and her gods you profess, but about the hermit in your backyard you know nothing. How foolish!

Rondangozi

Stop bickering Changamire! You've just been banished. Leave us now!

Chemusango

I don't fight physical battles as if there's a scarcity of curses where I come from. (*A sly smile*) But I like happy endings, like an epic romance that culminates in a pompous marriage ceremony. (*Points at Rondangozi then at the king*) Today visit your nearest and dearest, watch the sun go down and gorge yourselves with scrumptious food. I contest not the banishment, but tomorrow a journey awaits the two of you. (*Slight pause*) Should I stray into any village whip me senseless in the market-place. When you tire, burn me alive. Cast what remains of me to the dogs of the city.

Zunzanyika

You further sentence yourself severely. Rondangozi and the warriors will bear witness.

Chemusango rubs his hands together and stretches the right one to Rondangozi who stares at it hesitantly

Chemusango

(*Hand still out-stretched for a hand shake*)

A hand shake would be proper, Rondangozi. This is a solemn settlement in which you relieve the Rozvi. It is a momentous occasion worth celebrating.

Rondangozi demurs then takes his hand. They shake hands firmly. Impatiently, the king crosses to them and in the same manner shakes the hermit's hand.

Zunzanyika
(Curtly, and accompanied by a dismissive gesture)
Now be gone, hermit! The banishment is already effective!

Chemusango
(Bows in mock humility and waves at them as he steps backwards)
Yes, Changamire, I'll take my leave now. What business do I have with a *n'anga* and his king?

Exit Chemusango. The king and the medium are left staring at his point of exit. Behind them the four bodyguard warriors lying prostrate rise wearily, picking up their weapons.

Curtain.

Scene 3

6th Day. Morning. King Zunzanyika's courtyard.

(A unique drumbeat sounds thrice before the curtain goes up to reveal a deserted courtyard with stools and benches scattered about. Enter Kapingu after a while looking confounded. He wanders aimlessly for a moment then sits on a stool, hunched over and thoughtful. Enter Makeredza shortly. The two shake hands. Makeredza sits on a stool and as the two clap hands in greeting, a cow moos and a bull bellows off-stage.)

Kapingu

I came as soon as I heard the drumbeat, Kapingu. Who summons the elders?

Makeredza

It cannot be anyone else except Changamire.

Kapingu

It cannot be him; the Lion is gravely ill. You can't know it because you travelled the past four days. Most clansmen left Ibwe soon after the hermit's visit – a commendable precautionary measure.

Makeredza

What ails him?

Kapingu

I didn't see him, but his young brother, Dombo, is telling clansmen that life has left his left side. One side of his body is now redundant. He says speech has deserted him and he labours to breathe.

Makeredza

(Mournfully)

It's that accursed stiffness that arrests a man's body - often irreversible and fatal.

Kapingu

It came upon him the evening of the abominable day when Chemusango emerged from the forest. This is the ailment's sixth day. Dombo says nothing can save him now.

Makeredza

Can't Rondangozi do something?

Kapingu

O! So you haven't heard? *(Shakes his head and sighs)* These are warlike

times, Makeredza. Rondangozi is dead.
Makeredza gasps and gapes his mouth wide open.
But astoundingly upon him are signs of both life and death.

Makeredza
Have you become a riddle-peddler, Kapingu?

Kapingu
That's the dreadful truth. Something evil was bound to happen.
Indeed evil roamed the length and breath of the village. Many
infants died on their mother's bosoms. Reports say they developed
a high fever, fizzled in no time and then died. Cattle too perished.

Makeredza
I learnt about the infants and the cattle. But about the medium,
you're breaking terrible news to me. How did this come about?
Was it the stiffness too?

Kapingu
The whole thing is weird. I'm coming from viewing his body at
Matonjeni Shrine in the Matoba Hills. It's a horrific sight. His body
lies on its back on the large flat boulder near the mouth of *Mwari's*
cave. A few paces away his acolyte's body dangles from that shady
cork-tree. Both Rondangozi and Gagi are dead.
Makeredza whistles softly, sorrowfully, clutching his head.
The horror of it is unbearable. The surrounding trees are already
laden with staring hungry vultures that won't be scared away. The
scene like some sadistic grotto or joke in bad taste! But it's real. I
saw it firsthand.

Makeredza
He was overpowered. I knew he would be. Those who stayed
behind said the hermit spoke boldly, his words enamoured of an
evil intent. Our Rondangozi spoke timidly, like a little girl tasting
courtship.

Kapingu
They say there was an evil romance in Chemusango's words,
especially when he bid them farewell.

Makeredza
You said Rondangozi seemed alive and dead. What did you mean?

Kapingu
It's mind-bogging. There's a fervent debate at the shrine as we
speak. His eyes are open, gazing at the sky. Blood trickles out of

his mouth and nostrils… in fact it trickles out of every orifice on his body. Old scars on his body are bleeding too.

Makeredza

What kind of disease is that?

Kapingu

Who knows? I touched him, there's some warmth in his ribs. But I couldn't detect a heartbeat. He doesn't seem to be breathing. It's only his fingertips and toes that have taken the hue of death – pale, ashen and stiff like dry sticks.

Makeredza

This is bizarre… very bizarre. What did others conclude?

Kapingu

It's a gathering of spineless elders mainly from the western village. I'm the only one who touched the body. The rest looked at it from a distance like children marvelling at a python. While I was at it someone shouted that the medium's pharynx moved.

Makeredza

If it moved then he is alive, no doubt.

Kapingu

I didn't see it move, Makeredza. Another elder quickly said the shadow a vulture cast on the corpse had tricked the man's eyes.

Makeredza

You're an elder, Kapingu. This isn't the first corpse you've seen in your life. We know there's no death in life, and life in death.

Kapingu

My eyes have seen many dead people. I've had the sad task of declaring many kinsmen dead. But today, if I must be honest, I examined a body and couldn't make up my mind. As the only one who had the nerve to feel the body, I commanded some respect and attention. I declared him dead, then on second thoughts alive, then dead again as if I had lost my faculties. It continued like that until some elderly rogue scolded my dead mother with obscenities. That's when I left because tempers were flaring. (*Pauses and looks at his hands*) I rushed to a brook and thoroughly washed my hands. I had started to feel a strange sensation in my fingers. Perhaps my mind was beginning to create perceptions from the horror of the scene.

25

Makeredza

This is unprecedented. (*Reminiscing*) If someone declares him dead, a living person is then buried. If he is declared alive the declarer should be prepared to tend him back to full life. Tell me about Gagi.

Kapingu

His corpse swings from the sacred cork-tree. His neck is broken. The acolyte appears to be silently watching over his dead master below. All the signs of death by hanging are upon him. Both corpses were discovered today.

Makeredza

Rondangozi could be alive; a corpse doesn't haemorrhage, not at all. The warmth in his ribcage is indicative of life.

Kapingu

But he wasn't breathing. He had no heartbeat. The medium had been missing for about five days, which might mean he had lain in that position all these days. If the hermit's witchcraft didn't get him then starvation did.

Enter Chapwanya bearing a battle-axe.

Chapwanya

(*Wielding the axe, warlike*)

If Rondangozi rises from that boulder I'll hack him to shreds. (*Holds the axe aloft*) For this reason alone I'm carrying this axe.

Makeredza

Sit down, Chapwanya. Why do you turn against a dead man?

Chapwanya

That man, a charlatan according to the hermit, was the worst hoax that ever happened to the Rozvi. Now he's paid with his life.

Makeredza

You don't have to speak like an evil spirit. Rondangozi was Rozvi, a clansman. How could another Rozvi cherish the death of a brother?

Chapwanya

(*Momentarily mimics a war dance swinging the axe*)

You fuel my fury, Makeredza. The charlatan was dishonourable. He hoodwinked our foolhardy Changamire and clansmen into believing we were all under the protection of his charms. Yet he was a miserable *n'anga* who couldn't even protect himself. I'm a bitter man. This deception cost me an infant child – my dear Tongai, three cows and a bull.

Makeredza
You have my condolence, Chapwanya. May the guardian spirits wipe your tears away by giving you many sons.

Kapingu
May calves rain in your cattle pen.

Chapwanya sets a stool and sits on it.

Chapwanya
Over thirty children and about a dozen adults died throughout the eight villages. The deceased were mostly from homesteads alongside the path Chemusango used on his way to the courtyard and back. When he passed near my homestead Tongai was suckling at his mother's breast in the cooking-hut. Innocent blood just has to be avenged or I'll lose my self-esteem. If I had what it takes I would pursue the monstrous hermit.

Kapingu
(*Wringing his hands*)
Did you hear the king ails gravely?

Chapwanya
Changamire is dead, Chinake. You elders should know better. The death of a king is concealed for some days, that is tradition. Officially they say he is ill. If ill, where is he receiving treatment? The royal compound lulls in inactivity. The king and four of his most senior wives are not here. It's rumoured half of his body is stiffened. Don't listen to that. Changamire is dead.

The elders share snuff and begin to sniff. Enter Gundu and Nyamaropa conversing. They stop at the edge on the courtyard.

Gundu
(*Putting a hand on Nyamaropa's shoulder*)
It was Gagi who discovered his master dead this morning. Gagi sounded the alarm. I was one of the first clansmen to arrive at the shrine. There lay Rondangozi on the boulder, dead, like some war hero brought home and lying-in-state, except that ironically this was a villain. What confounded me was the bleeding… like water seeping out of a saturated field. And the eyes! The eyes seemingly watching the clouds!

Nyamaropa

And Gagi was alive then, you were with him?

Gundu

Gagi was alive. He's the one who showed us the body. He said he hadn't seen the medium in four days. I guessed Gagi was holed up in his homestead all these days in anticipation of tragedy. When he came out of hiding he went to the shrine and found his master on the boulder.

Nyamaropa

But a cruel thing you did. You should have restrained Gagi from taking his life.

Gundu

Gagi didn't look or sound suicidal. We were under some blinding spell, I think. (*With the aid of gestures*) There we were, looking down at the body and arguing. There was Gagi, moving around restlessly and inconsolable until everyone tired of minding him. The last time I saw him alive he was sitting under the cork-tree behind us. At the time, the dispute whether Rondangozi was alive or dead, raged. A short while later we heard a sound behind us, and saw him up the tree, swinging. His head hung at an awkward angle. It was indisputable that he was dead.

Nyamaropa

Such an abomination has never happened. To think it happened in the hallowed shrine of our most revered god sends a chill in my intestines. That oracular place of quietude, peace and solitude has been defiled by the blood of its minister. *Mwari* could be communicating something to us through this happening. (*Thoughtfully, slowly*) Two dead bodies in a holy shrine surrounded by a gathering of stubborn vultures! (*Shakes his head*) Have we been called to bury the dead?

Gundu

It's taboo for us to touch such bodies. A non-kinsman has to be found to perform the abominable task without risk.

The two proceed to greet the elders already seated as the rest of the Council arrives from different directions. For a moment the courtyard is abuzz with salutations and clapping, but the atmosphere is subdued. Enter Dombo shortly in a matching high turban, a toga and a flaring cloth around his waist wound into a legged gird. His feet are in exotic sandals. Copper bangles cover his wrists and ankles. The effect is Arabic. The elders still standing find stools and settle down upon his appearance. Dombo stands beside the throne.

Dombo

Elders, we are all thunderstruck. But let me express my heartfelt condolences to you and your families for the unfathomable loss of family members and relatives as well as the cattle that you have all lost. Most of you have been to the shrine and will testify to the inconceivable occurrence there. However, I didn't summon you here to discuss a mystery, for that is beyond human faculties and must await the return of the diviners. But as elders we could collectively put our feet down and declare Rondangozi either died or alive. This we must do urgently to avert a brawl at the shrine; hooligans schooled in hostilities are bent on settling the controversy with fist-fights. A mob is gathering in the shrine as are gawking vultures' on the trees around Maboba Hills. You sit in the Council on the strength of your achievements. To hooligans civil war is a glorious achievement. I'm appealing to your better judgments to find a solution to this crisis within a crisis before the state slides into a foolish civil war. In our day we shouldn't allow war to start from a place of serenity or the wishes of monumental failures to prevail.

Pauses and looks around, adjusting the toga. The elders nod in agreement. Kapingu inspects his hands and wrings them briefly before messaging his arms. Thereafter he can be observed fanning himself and wringing his hands occasionally.

Though I'm Changamire Zunzanyika's younger brother and heir-apparent, I don't stand here to deputise for him. I stand here as a family spokesman tasked to accede to your counsel and to keep you informed of any developments, especially as regards the Rozvi Lion. I regret to inform the Council of his grave illness.

Chinake

Where have you put the king?

Dombo

We took him to the land of our legendary cousins, the Ndau. Four of his senior wives accompanied him. A renowned medicine-man took the king and his wives into his custody. The rest of us were turned away for reasons best known to the medicine-man himself. We believe he sought to minimise contagion.

Chapwanya shakes his head and looks away in disgust.

I'm privileged to announce that that grotesque hermit was finally banished. You're all being called upon to enforce the banishment. We've been terrorised for far too long and have been agonised beyond measure. That brusque character is to be stoned to pulp and set ablaze on sight. This instruction must reach every village in Urozviland.

The elders clap their hands and nod in support.

Allow me to revert to the issue at hand. Rondangozi lies inert in the shrine of his god. Those convinced he is alive are free to collect him from that boulder. Rise and do so now.

No one rises. The elders just exchange glances.

I'm not going to ask those who think he is dead to bury him. If he's dead then that's solid confirmation of a blackguardly spell on him. Refrain from touching the body. The incautious always perish; a river doesn't drown a coward. Let no clansman ever say we were accomplices in the murder of Rondangozi through complacency and negligence. We're all resolved that he's dead, which puts the matter to rest.

Makeredza

The corpses are in *Mwari's* shrine. Do we just look away? Is this not going to invite famine, bring on pestilenc or even war to our land?

Dombo

The Augur, the Soothsayer and the Sorcerer have all fled the arena. Mere men would be fools to touch those bodies. If indeed the medium wants to be buried he shall find a way of communicating it. There's no urgency, his head rests in comfort on Gagi, a pillow he made himself this morning.

Gundu

He lies-in-state on that boulder before his god whom he served continually all his life. But with Rondangozi gone, aren't we now spiritually naked?

Chinake

Perhaps we've always been naked. Perhaps now our nudity is covered. It's better to know you have no source of water than to take solace in a mirage.

Nyamaropa

Time will tell if we need a territorial medium or if we already have one whom we're banishing.

30

Chapwanya
Don't allude to that accursed wizard in my presence! Rondangozi isn't worth remembering. Alive, he failed to protect us! Dead, he continues to give us problems by haemorrhaging! (*Rises*) The fifteen diviners smelled this horror. Your brother in his foolish wisdom refused to listen to them; otherwise protective rituals would have been conducted.
Murmur of concurrence from the elders. Kapingu's actions are less hectic now. This meeting is a waste of time, just like all the other meetings we have had. If there're no further issues to discuss can we be dismissed? (*Sits*)

Dombo
It's retrogressive to be emotional when rationality is demanded. All of us have suffered loss one way or the other. My brother lies on his deathbed.

Makeredza
Perhaps you should tell us what became of the white-skins and their eight porters. Are they still in the pit?

Dombo
Changamire did as bidden by the diviners. Chikasha Forest is now their home. Warriors took them there on the accursed day. The decree is that they're not to set foot in Ibwe or in any of the villages. We all know what that forest harbours and who frequents it. If they survive beyond a month I shall burn my shrine and prostrate before their gods.

Chapwanya
(*Angrily*)
Changamire simply postponed a calamity.

Chinake
(*Rising*)
Your brother gave foreign gods residence in our kingdom! Since times ancestral the Rozvi have resisted deities the Egyptians, the Turks, and the Portuguese and others brought to us. Every clansman has his foreskin today as a constant reminder of our staunch denial of foreign gods. Why do you toy with a kingdom? (*Looks around him for support, then sits*)

31

Gundu

The dreams Dombolakochingwano aspired for this kingdom found their snag in Zunzanyika.

Dombo

Calm down, elders, I'm only a spokesman. The utterances of the mediums took precedence. Changamire didn't err. But rest assured Chikasha Forest will devour that bunch.

Makeredza

Foreigners are about to set fire to Urozviland, and all you say is: "Calm down, elders." If we're not careful, clansmen will be converted. Times have changed; the Rozvi have suffered much. Many could be eager to experiment with other gods.

Chinake

This meeting sours the heart. (*Rises*) Why is our counsel sought when it is never followed? Looking back, we've always been summoned, but none of our proposals was ever implemented. If ever, the implementation was vague, our resolutions having been grossly modified. I would rather spend time measuring my shadow. (*Walks away briskly. Exit Chinake*)

Makeredza

Zunzanyika is ill. You should be by his bedside, Dombo. He needs your reassurance that he'll live. But you're here chairing a useless meeting. If anything happens to him you shall be deemed guilty of insensitivity.

Gundu

We need a man of unimpeachable integrity and credibility to stand before us, not a lengthened shadow of Zunzanyika.

Dombo

What are you saying, Gundu?

Gundu

I won't be party to this fallacy (*Rises and makes for the exit, all the while gesturing his annoyance. Exit Gundu*)

Chapwanya

We're in a crisis. The last thing needful is for a fool to focus his strength on gaining power. A little reverence would have been proper; we're still mourning our children. (*Rises, the battle-axe in his hand*) If you placed any seriousness in us you'd have notified us of Changamire's death.

Dombo

He's alive, Chapwanya! Go to the land of the Ndau and discover for yourself!

Chapwanya

I bet my entire herd of cattle he's dead! You know it! I renounce my membership from this Council!

A moment of tense silence follows, Chapwanya and Dombo boring each other with their eyes. Kapingu slouches, then suddenly falls from his stool and begins to kick wildly, making gurgling sounds and clutching his neck with both hands. The elders rise in panic and look down helplessly at Kapingu. Dombo joins them. Suddenly Kapingu lies inert on his back in front of everyone. The elders exchange bewildered glances. Everyone draws back.

Curtain.

Act II

Scene 1

9th Day. Morning. Mission site; part of a cleared area in Chikasha Forest.

(Eight distinctively sloe-eyed black men in loincloths, the porters from Sofala, are working on the frame of a primitive hut in the background. About half of the frame is off-stage. All are wearing large, beaded copper earrings that touch their shoulders. Some are strapping the poles onto the frame, some are bringing poles and bark from off-stage, and others are de-barking the poles with machetes and adzes. All are engrossed in the work but singing discordantly:
Father Abraham had many sons!
Had many sons, Father Abraham!
I'm one of them!
So are you.....!
Large suitcases and wooden crates are stacked in a corner in the background. Two folded chairs rest against the stack. Enter a soiled Rev. Holbrook carrying a pole, which he passes to the men de-barking. He appraises the framing, yawns tiredly and fetches one of the two chairs. He sits quietly, the porters behind him. Enter Shannon Forrester bearing steaming tea on a tray, which she sets before him.)

Shannon

(To the porters, shouting over their singing)
Tea! Tea is ready, guys!
The porters excitedly shout 'tea!' both on and off-stage. Shannon points off-stage. Exit all the porters quickly in the direction indicated. The singing fades and dies. Shannon fetches the second chair and sits beside the Reverend. She fills and sweetens two cups. They converse over tea nursing their cups in their hands.

Shannon

(Appreciatively)
This tract of land is priceless. It rolls endlessly in all directions. (*A hand mimicking features*) It undulates into breath-taking loess plains; metamorphoses into overawing hills, then levels again only to knot into picturesque kopjes like jagged hands pointing at the sky. The valleys are Irish in their splendour. The ferns and the brooks induce a home-sickness.

Holbrook

You haven't said anything about the meadows.

Shannon

Oh, the meadows, Reverend! Untamed and inviting they stretch to the iridescent horizons. When you look in the distance, you notice that this part of the tract is mountain-circumscribed; a natural fortress indeed. Our Bronze Age pastoral warriors would have camped here permanently and slaughtered everybody. I could write an endless poem on this gift. This is the kind of land the Celts, the Romans, the Norwegians…everybody, died for.

Holbrook

Because Britain was tempting she endured repeated invasions from everybody. It brought with it devastation and enslavement. Thank God we aren't Vikings. (*Pause*) And God just gave us this virgin land, just like that (*Clicks his fingers*) From the pit, to land-owners; the quickest real estate transaction ever! No dime, no paperwork, no lawyers… this prodigality is manna!

Shannon

(*Looking about*)

The African birds and their orchestra! The fragrance of the flame-lily! What an untrammelled Eden to headquarter a church!

Holbrook

This blessing landed in our hands out of malice. This is Chikasha Forest, their supposed purgatory for swarthy spirits. For twenty-five kilometres in all directions there's neither village nor sign of human existence. This is where they dump stillborn babies, twins, albinos, dwarfs and such like. Anything considered evil ends up here.

Shannon

What a pity! An enlightened eye sees nothing but beautiful outcrops and virgin soil around. The pagan eye is blind to that. (*Pauses, the excitement deserting her abruptly*) The warriors who brought us here mentioned that that feared hermit of theirs frequents this forest.

Holbrook

In the native mind our fate is sealed.

Shannon

That man somehow unleashed death. Children and cattle are said to have died in large numbers, Reverend. What do you think of him?

Holbrook

Sister Shannon, the fear of the devil will get you nowhere. Think about the deceiver and you exalt him. I urge you to delight only in the fear of the Lord.

Shannon

It seems theology prepares us to preach to prostitutes, pimps and all sorts of villains. But now I'm of the opinion it does not adequately prepare evangelists for a one-on-one encounter with the devil.

Holbrook

Change the subject, Sister Shannon; without knowing it you've suddenly plunged into idolatry.

Shannon

(*Picking up the teapot*)

More tea, Reverend?

He holds out his cup, which she refills.

Holbrook

We've started with one hut, by tomorrow there'll be three – the humble birth of a great mission. An equally primitive one room-affair church will follow. But once we contact London and receive material, the primitive structures shall bow out. A cathedral, schools, a university, a public library, you name it, shall grace this land. I foresee the universities of London and Oxford exchanging staff and modules with us. Chronicle all these things, Sister Shannon. Future generations shall read about our dreams and marvel at God.

Shannon

Oh, I nearly forgot to tell you. Ferenado went to the village yesterday and returned in the evening.

Holbrook

Though the ban is against the two of us, I wonder if it's advisable for him to return to the villages. He could get killed. What did he bring back from the village?

Shannon

If you could hear everything from him the better. The gyre continues to widen, twists and turns. (*Cups a hand around her mouth and calls off-stage*) Ferenado! Ferenado!

Enter Ferenado shortly, a large tin teacup in his hand.

Sorry to disturb your tea break, Ferenado, but the Reverend is interested in your story. Sit down, please.

Ferenado sits cross-legged, sips his tea and sets the cup before him.

You'll excuse Ferenado's Rozvi. It's haphazard; he learnt it from the brief contact he had with fellow-porters prying the Ibwe-Sofala route.

Holbrook
I'm listening, Brother Ferenado.

Ferenado
(With an excess of gestures)
Yesterday, me, Drao Ferenado, return to pit. Drao Ferenado looking for one of his bangles. My father give it to me when he is alive… breathing, but dying. The bangle is a copper bangle. This bangle from my father bring luck and protect me. Me loosed it in the pit. Me go there to look for it.
Ferenado looks at Rev. Holbrook to see if he should continue. The Reverend nods.
Ferenado return to pit. Look, look bangle. Nothing. Look every corner of pit. No Bangle. People see Ferenado, but no trouble. People say men from Sofala good men. Our women, no touch; our cattle, no touch. But white-skins danger not wanted. People say if white-skins return to village spear, spear. *(Mimes stabbing twice)*

Holbrook
I'm aware of the ban. Any breach and we're dead.

Shannon
Tell him everything you told me, Brother Ferenado.

Ferenado
Trouble medium and his snuff-man died. No Buried. People tremble, tremble bewitched! Bewitched! Trouble medium no trouble again. But people happy? No. *(Lowers voice)* Whispers, whispers. Chemusango… Chemusango. Some say Chemusango good man. Some shake head, say Chemusango evil man. *(To Shannon)* Anything else, madam?

Shannon
(Spurring him on)
Come on, Ferenado… the visitor.

Ferenado
A man arrive, mirror of you, Reverend. People say he arrive yesterday of yesterday counting from yesterday.
Holbrook smiles and shakes his head. Shannon laughs.

Shannon
He says a white man who looks like you came to Ibwe. The visitor had arrived the day before Ferenado's visit to the village.

Holbrook
Oh, yes. Go on, Brother Ferenado.

39

Ferenado
(*Continues actively*)
Elephant, he shoot on arriving. Rhinoceros, he shoot. Ivory! Ivory! Bring! Bring! Ferenado ask: (*Calmly, head tilted*) "This man man of God?" People answer: "No. This man no man of God. This man hunter in love with ivory." So this man no trouble. Elders no gathering. Everyone eat elephant and rhinoceros meat.

Holbrook
(*Thoughtfully*)
A white hunter and ivory trader is in the village… most likely a Briton. The man is cunning and already enjoys some popularity.

Shannon
Ferenado said the king's young brother, Dombo, has taken the newcomer into his custody. He brought in two large wagons, each pulled by a team of four horses. Two men from across the Limpopo drove the wagons. The wagons carried baggage and a dismantled wooden house. The newcomer rode on the ninth horse… a very well-to-do man.

Holbrook
(*Ponderous monologue*)
A bourgeois. What is a bourgeoisie hunter doing in the heart of undomesticated Africa? (*To Shannon*) The cabin means he is here to stay. Anything else of interest, Brother Ferenado?

Ferenado
White-skin give Dombo one horse already. Dombo no rest, ride up and down all the time. Children play inside homestead because Dombo ride very fast up and down the village.

Holbrook
The two wagon drivers, what tribe were they?

Ferenado
Wagon drivers baVenda. Strong men, tall and the baVenda men angry all the time. People shake head and say these baVenda men killer bees.

Holbrook
A hazy picture is taking shape. (*Cogitatively slow*) A rich hunter landed somewhere along the vast coastline of the Cape Colony. He probably knew about the Zulu and the Afrikaners, and avoided them; otherwise his wagons wouldn't have reached this place. From

40

a Venda chief he managed to obtain or hire the two wagon drivers. He knew with profound exactitude where he was going.

Shannon

How can you be certain of that, Reverend?

Holbrook

This region is fraught with marauding tribes. He circumvented all of them. He couldn't have missed the Zulu, the Boers, the Tswana, the Luvedu and others, then crossed the Limpopo and continued to miss the Ndebele, all by chance. This man is a meticulous strategist who issued from a planning room, that's my speculation. If he's indeed British we ought to be celebrating an addition to our number, but I have this premonition about him.

A long silence.

I shall need an hour or two of solitude, Sister Shannon. (*Rises*)

Shannon

God be with you, Sir.

Holbrook

God be with you, too.

Exit Rev. Holbrook troubled.

Shannon

Thanks Ferenado, we definitely required such information.

Booming singing comes from off-stage: 'Father Abraham…' Enter the other porters singing to man their former positions. Shannon waves at Ferenado who drains his teacup, sets it down, goes to the frame being put together and joins in the singing. For a while Shannon is thoughtful. She rises and crosses over to the foreground where she kneels to pray. Enter Chemusango dressed as before, the calabashes on his sides. Upon his appearance the porters panic, yell and scurry off, exiting. Shannon turns her head and is petrified. Looking away, she remains kneeling, her eyes bulging. Chemusango halts in the background and casually appraises the framing, his hands behind him.

Chemusango

(*Nodding self-assuredly and facing the frame*)

This endeavour is blessed. First I see an atypical compound of huts around a large structure of poles and grass. Within a season I foresee magnificent, sprawling constructions, of extravagant designs and timeless durability, replacing the huts. In all directions they sprawl while others aspire to touch the sky. In the buildings I see calabashes filling, drop by drop, with words, words, words –

words of knowledge and wisdom. (*Turns and looks at her*) This is your season of favour.

Shannon
(*Still on her knees but looking away. Tremulous*)
What do you want?

Chemusango
Fear not, white daughter. I come in peace, and my peace I offer you. I'm on your side; therefore I can't have come to hurt you. (*Slowly crosses to her*) This is Chikasha, the domain of vengeful spirits and hissing vipers from which I shall protect you. I've come to render prophetic encouragement. Sons of strangers shall build your walls. Kings shall minister to you. The gates of this place shall not close.

He stops a pace from her, but looks her over as she turns and looks up at him.
Misinterpret my benevolence as evil to your own detriment. Have you ever asked yourselves why the lions and the leopards of this forest cower on seeing you? Innumerable roving elephants smell your presence and are bothered by your intrusion. But every animal is under instruction to keep away from you. I'm your friend, sojourner, and I like happy endings. (*Looks down at her*) Enough of this act of homage. Rise and take a seat.

He points at the chairs. Surprised to find she had been kneeling all along, she rises, puts on a brave face and stands akimbo in defiance, facing him.
(*Skyward*) The four winds carry me everywhere. As the white stork flies, so do I.

He suddenly shrieks and jerks simultaneously, startling Shannon who recoils and brings her hands up fearfully, then composes herself again.
The northern wind has taken me across lands and seas. On the land of gloomy confers I land; the land of the elm, the hazel and the alder. Dense evergreens surround a dwelling of stone and mortar facing west. Standing at the gate, to the left in the yard, enormous yew-trees planted by the hand of men. To the right, an aged solitary oak-tree. The walls were once ochreous yellow, but have faded over the years.

Shannon
(*Clutches her chest in shock*)
Oh, God! My father's manor house in   England!

Chemusango
Your Father lies almost lifeless on a bed. Smoke and disease have wasted his chest.

Shannon
(*Breathless*)
That's my father... Bryn Hudson Forrester. How do you know
these things?

Chemusango
Sit down, young lady, or have I overstayed my welcome.
She sits in one of the chairs.
Why did you turn your back on a parent so wasted? Your mother,
Lucy, prays for your return. She denies herself food. She had
found you a gentlemanly suitor. Had she not voiced her reservations
about this sojourn?
She begins to sob
Cry all you want, young lady, but Phibion of Streatham is crying
miserably. He wanted to marry you – a resourceful young man
pretty like a woman. But you spurned him for this land bought at
no price. Cry the more. Drown that heartless heart in tears. In vain
you shall sail home. I see them burying your father and mother as
the sea buffets and toss your vessel.
*She quakes and cries, shoulders heaving, feet stamping. He looks at her
indifferently and crosses briskly from the foreground to the frame of the hut in
the background. She quietens and watches him, rising hesitantly. In the
background he halts, his back to her.*

Shannon
Sir, can't you do something to save my parents?
He turns and faces her.

Chemusango
My clansmen see me as a grotesque personage. For the sake of
my heritage I live on wild honey and the milk of baboons. (*Taps
the gourds hanging at his sides. He uncorks both. From one he pours out a
small measure of milk, from the other honey, and corks them*) The bee
stings me. The suckling baboon slaps me. (*Pause*) This site is a
ground bird's nest, but I didn't hurt you.

Shannon
Are you going to do something for my parents?

Chemusango
The eyes of the Perfect One are on you to give you an expected
happy ending. Bryn and Lucy shall live. I declare it!

Shannon
(*Smiles*)
But how can I be sure of their recovery? Confirm it by oath.

Chemusango
Men verily swear by the greater. An oath of confirmation is to them an end to all strife. Believe the immutability of the power of the spiritual realm.

Shannon
What then is your reward?

Chemusango
None whatsoever. And under no condition do I favour you.

Shannon
I don't know how to thank you, Sir. But does it mean I should stay?

Chemusango
The sting has been taken out of the scorpion for you. Phibion of Streatham is already married. But on this ground I see suitors of royal blood from far flung places and overseas contending for your hand in marriage. They shall come in carriages, on horseback and on camels, all attended by servants overburdened with gifts. Within two years you shall wed here in the presence of your parents.

Shannon
Honestly, I don't know how to thank you.

Chemusango
I must take my leave; the solemnity of solitude beckons me. My regards to the teacher of divinity. Outside that, utter no word.
Exit Chemusango swiftly. For a long moment Shannon stares in the direction he took, and then falls on her knees to pray.

Curtain.

Scene 2

12th Day. Afternoon. Chapwanya's stockaded homestead: backyard.

(A small mound of earth, a child's grave is in the backyard. The place is unkempt, wooden stools, a drum and broken pots etc, lie about amid grass and dirt. Chinake on his feet winnows grain, Makeredza on his knees grinds groundnuts/corn, and Gundu pounds maize in a knee-high mortar using a pestle. The men absorbed in their work and sweat, the noise of their activities mingles like some orchestra. After a while Gundu stops to catch his breath, the others follow suit one after the other.)

Gundu
(Resting the pestle in the mortar and rubbing his palms together)
Who ever thought that a day would come when we would turn into women? My back is sore. Now I see the importance of women and the permanence of comradeship.

Makeredza
We would be quite a spectacle. If we're discovered, rumour would have it that Chapwanya married us.
They laugh.

Chinake
The stockade and the mango trees hide us from prying eyes; otherwise we would've attracted spectators. Between tree trunks and gaps in the stockade we see the world, but the world doesn't see us.

Gundu
It boggles the mind to think that the location of an infant's grave can not only cause an uproar but lead to divorce. Now a man of standing leads the life of a widower. Fellow-men must assist him with chores.

Chinake
He's becoming an apparition, perhaps of the order of Chemusango.

Makeredza
But pragmatically speaking, Chapwanya erred most horrifically. *(Pointing at the grave)* A grave in one's backyard is taboo. The grave potentially invites death to the neighbourhood, which is why the neighbours are not amused.

Chinake

Exile is preferable to this anomaly.

Gundu

Elders, are you confident of the rationality of the clansman we are assisting with chores?

Makeredza

Chapwanya suffers from one disease, which is abruptness in decision making. Otherwise he has a tall record of bravery and frankness. Over sixty head of cattle and eight well-fed wives make him a man of achievement. This one disease is his sole weakness.

Chinake

If you thought him somehow insane, why did you honour his invitation?

Gundu

Curiosity, Chinake, curiosity. He openly renounced his membership from the Council. A man of his calibre cannot just renounce such prestige for the sake of it. Since then I've been speculating. Perhaps today I'll hear his mind.

Makeredza

I hope for an opportunity to coax him into exhuming the child. For normalcy's sake he must be reburied far from the villages. I also want to hear his mind in these times of distress.

Chinake

I came because always, one listens to Chapwanya with compassion, with worry, and with fear. However, our disgruntlement needs a shepherd. Chapwanya is a resolute man; that's why I came.

Makeredza

(*Nodding concurrence*)

Our discontent has to be breeched for it to be useful. My heart tells me he could take us out of this quagmire.

Gundu

Is your heart sure he isn't the quagmire?

Chinake

(*Looking off-stage*)

There he comes.

The men resume pounding, grinding and winnowing. Enter Chapwanya carrying a large gourd spilling millet beer, and a beer-drinking ladle. Gundu relieves him of the gourd and sets it down. Makeredza and Chinake abandon their work, pick stools and sit, wiping sweat. All sit, with Chapwaya close to the grave.

Chapwanya

This brew I personally prepared for our meeting. I invited you here, to a meeting, but out of consideration you elected to perform these menial chores first despite your age and stature, aware that my family deserted me. Well, in a crisis men bend while women break. May the spirit-elders protect you from the fangs of the cobra.

Chinake

May your wives know no rest until they return with your children.

Chapwanya

The chores and your prayers humble me. Quench your thirst, elders, as we talk; the chores can wait.

Chapwanya fills the ladle, takes a token sip and hands it to Chinake, who gulps it empty immediately. Thus, the men gulp from the ladle as Chapwanya talks.

Thank you for coming. Only one man couldn't make it due to a disarming illness in his family, otherwise he would have been here. His name I shall not disclose for his protection. (*Pensively*) There's a sombre novelty in Ibwe. We buried our children and burnt the carcasses of our cattle. When we thought it was over, Kapingu succumbed before the Council of Elders. We've also seen a clansman celebrating his brother's death. And the vulgarity thickens; the same clansman enjoys horse riding as his brother's body lies before embalmers. A passing hunter of unknown reputation and unverifiable origins becomes the proud owner of our ancestral land. In the middle of all this a king's death is hushed to the elders. *Off-stage galloping noise attracts their attention. All rise and point in awe, mouths agape, tracking a fast horse-rider with their fingers.*

Makeredza

There goes Dombo on horseback! Ahe! Ahe! Ahe! The speed! *It takes a while before they lose sight of him off-stage.*

Chinake

What a rare spectacle!

Gundu

He rides that horse like a maniac.

Makeredza

(*Fearfully*)

He might fall and break his neck.

Chapwanya
Let him fall and break every one of his bones!

Makeredza
Aye! You hate him that much, Chapwanya?

Chapwanya
I hate excitable characters. We're under siege and the heir-apparent embarks on a riding spree. That horse has obsessed him ever since he received it. The hunter gave Dombo that horse on account of his excitability.

All sit, shaking their heads.

Gundu
Let him rejoice. He has ten wives to inherit, and countless cattle, goats and sheep. All those exotic gifts by which the merchants expressed their homage with ... the rolls of calico and silk, the lengths of tapestry, the guns, the prayer books no one can read... all that is his inheritance.

Chinake
You left out the grandest of the gifts, that four-post bedstead hung with damask curtains the Portuguese brought.

Gundu
Oh, yes; that was soon after Zunzanyika's coronation seven years ago when wave after wave of itinerant traders visited Ibwe. In those days Arabic and Portuguese merchants vied to outdo each other in homage, and monopolise trade. Gifts of all shapes and sizes landed at Zunzanyika's feet.

Chinake
The bedstead nearly did the trick for the Portuguese had the diviners' not intervened and condemned bribery and bias.

Makeredza
They also ordered that the gates to the royal court be shut for they were now ajar to dubious foreigners. No other Changamire had been so welcoming to foreigners.

Chapwanya
Before this clown is king his door is already wide-open to foreigners. Clansmen of valour in Ibwe watch this riding in silence, and are being tortured by it. Dombo will definitely pursue his brother's policies of doom.

Makeredza

I'm hard-pressed between castigating Changamire and praising him. At times my mind convinces me that he was or is a man of equity, and, equally, I thought him too porous.

Chapwanya

What is your assessment, Chinake?

Chinake

Slavish adherence to mediums is the only assurance for the Rozvi's survival. However, I suppose Changamire is dead and cannot make amends now. Foul-mouthing a reposing clansman is uncouth and uncustomary. In peace he must journey.

Chinake receives a full ladle from Gundu and drinks.

Chapwanya

(*Diplomatically*)

It satisfies me that I'm conferencing with notable thinkers; the thinker shall rouse the warrior to a frenzy. I refrain from thinking I could've been wrong when I handpicked you, my conviction spurred by your protests six days ago. Chagrin became your countenances. (*Slight pause*) Changamire is dead; let there be no doubt in anyone's mind. That he ails is propaganda for idiots. This is the eleventh day since he fell ill. Anytime now the royal crier shall sound the drum, and mourning can begin in earnest.

Chinake

If indeed dead, then Changamire has lain on the bier for far too long now. The maggots from his body have since died in their pots.

Gundu

His body fluids must have been put in ceramic Arabic jars in honour of his foreign tastes. These must have dried, too, by now. On that bier the skin of a black ox shrouding his body has dried, shrunk and pinioned the mummy.

Makeredza

By now the corpse should have left the cave of the embalmer to lie-in-state. Then when every tear is shed and wailing has been reduced to inaudible whispers, the mummy ought to be discreetly entombed.

Chinake

But a territorial medium must preside at every stage. Perhaps Chemusango will officiate by default.

Makeredza

No mourners would come near the royal compound.

Chapwanya

Elders, spiritual intrigues are beyond us. The diviners fled. The age of thinkers has begun. An impoverishing spirit has crept into us. Instead of gaining territories we're donating land. You're aware that five days ago another wanderer came. The Council wasn't consulted about his fate. The next thing you know, the arrival's gun is going off all the time and elephants and rhinoceros are falling in large numbers.

Gundu

The white-skin shoots without missing. He's dangerous and looks it.

Chapwanya

(Continuing)

You ask probing questions, but clansmen look away because of the meat in their mouths. Before you understand what is happening you learn that the alien has buried Rondangozi and his acolyte, and is being celebrated. You're about to verify such an absurdity, but already events on the ground have overtaken you; the celebrity has given Dombo a horse and is staying at his homestead.

Chinake

The next shocker is waking up to see smoking pyres in the distance. On close inspection I realise they were barbecues and bonfires on a vast acreage of fertile loam soils. An elephant's carcass is being skinned and quartered. Excited clansmen are already roasting another. The fools are feasting and clearing a vast piece of land and every tree, including our revered cork-tree, is falling. Next you hear that Dombo has unilaterally given the alien land on the periphery of the village.

Chapwanya

Dombo has decreed that all ivory be sold to the alien.

Makeredza

The white-skin is giving miserly payments. All ivory has been ordered out of homesteads. Refusal to sell and possession of the tusks have been declared criminal. A pit of adders is being dug for non-compliers.

Chinake

The two baVenda men who drove his wagons are enforcing the decree… ruthless men they are. Armed with guns and sjamboks, these men search the homesteads of hunters and ivory stockists, and confiscate their findings. Faceless sons of this soil give these brutes information in the dead of the night. The beatings have been horrible. A man is brutalised in front of his family until he groans and howls.

Makeredza

These brutes must be stopped.

Chapwanya

The shameless horse-rider is the fiend responsible for all this. He has turned his back on his brother's corpse, now he flays the Rozvi alive.

Gundu

Something must have crept into Dombo. His brothers who send him to address the elders must be giving him a false sense of kingship.

Chapwanya

Nobody sends him to address anybody. Everything is a concoction. The merry-maker has begun campaigning for the throne. In his speeches he has become solicitous. He encourages with a smile dunderheads who greet him in kingly totemic thanksgiving.

Chinake

I pitied him for his lack of self-restraint when he said his brother lay on a deathbed. Essentially he was saying: 'My brother won't rise from that bed, I'm the next king.' Why would an heir-apparent tell a gathering of elders that he is the heir-apparent?

Chapwanya
(Stirring the beer with the ladle)
A scrupulous clansman, neither cruel nor vindictive, should be elevated to that throne. (*Fills the ladle and gives it to Makeredza*) Changamire's negligence led to my son's death. Now I'm cautious enough to open my eyes as to who shall ascend that throne. (*Pointing*) This grave a constant reminder that I should be vigilant in my resolve….a constant call to action. I must avenge my Tongai, then exhume and rebury him normally only when he's avenged.

Gundu
Aren't you abusing your dead child, Chapwanya?

Makeredza
I thought so, too. Besides, graves enshrine the perils associated with death. They're to be avoided except for rituals. Occult powers hover over graves. The cautious journeyed to Chikasha Forest where they dumped the corpses on windswept fells or wedged them in crevices. Graves ought to be far from home. The neighbours are spooked.

Chapwanya
I'm a bitter man, elders. Today there's hardly any mention of the Amandabili. They invaded and occupied Guruuswa – our endless grasslands. For thirty-five years now they have been sitting quietly in our backyard having massacred our kith and kin. No one talks about it today as though the slaughter never happened. It's as though part of our land isn't under occupation.

Chinaka
The savannah grasslands were taken after a terrible carnage. But it's best to let alone the war-cravers from across the Limpopo. Beyond that river come devils. As it is, only two baVenda men are causing havoc in Ibwe. What about a formidable army of demonic *impis*!

Makeredza
I hate talking about the Amandabili. I lost many relatives in that raid thirty-five years ago. (*Mournfully*) Many were captured and adopted. Their names and totems were changed to Zulu.
A brief contemplative silence.

Chapwanya
Instead of Changamire preparing the warrior for war, he learnt about foreign divinities. He knew about almost every ancient city under the sun. By leaving the doors of his court ajar to outsiders he was foolish. But the merchants deliberately heightened this foolishness with knowledge Zunzanyika had no use for or could not. Had he employed this knowledge undoubtedly he would've restored Rozvi pride soon after his coronation. Knowledge lying idle in the head is an unnecessary burden.

Gundu

When the Amandabili were consolidating their positions in Guruuswa, Changamire occupied himself with Portuguese whisky. Drunk, he would babble about an empire called Ottoman, the grandeur of the Egyptian pyramids, and many other impertinent things.

Chapwanya

Now he's dead, but his spirit won't go. In Dombo he's raising his head again in a spectral feat. The horse-rider shouldn't be allowed to edge towards the throne.

Makeredza

Our anger is stirred; our repulsion of Dombo is heightened. You're an irrefutable man of war and substance. Are you eyeing the throne, Chapwanya?

Chapwanya
(Smiles and rises)

In our warrior days the four of us enjoyed a heartfelt comradeship. We waged war shoulder to shoulder, each an eye and shield for the other, thus, we saved one another in many campaigns. Are there any remnants of that old comradeship in you? A king is an investment. We're getting old, but that doesn't exempt us from leaving a memorial in this land. I need heroes to stand by me so that together we can prevail in investing wisely.

Chinake

Wresting kingship from an heir-apparent has tragic consequences. Frankly, you aren't everyone's eye. Whom did you have in mind?

Chapwany

Of your allegiance I must be certain before disclosure. I must protect the would-be investment. *(Strolls to the grave thoughtfully. Looking down at it)* I'll ask you to return to your homesteads to consider. Tomorrow at about the same time I'll strike a merry drumbeat. To those who come I shall make the disclosure for their approval. But as I stand beside my child's grave I need to warn you. My discontent I've revealed. Now beware of becoming my arch enemies. By the bones in this grave I swear this day that traitors will fall together with the cowards of this land.

Gundu

You threaten us unnecessarily, Chapwanya. Personally, death is a scarecrow in a tree. If I happen to return tomorrow discount the threat of death as my motive. I've never given death a second thought in my adult life.

Makeredza

We'll go to our homes and consider. I trust no shameful day will come when we'll have to hunt one another as traitors or, worse still, as intending perpetrators of treason. Both are punishable summarily.

Chinake

But whether tomorrow we continue as comrades or foes, we must finish the chores at hand. Come and sit down; your standing there overbears the child, sombre utterances unsettle his spirit. Let the child rest.

Chapwanya joins them and shakes their hands before sitting. The men rise quietly. Chinake returns to winnowing; Makeredza to grinding, and Gundu to pounding. The orchestra rises again. Chapwanya stares at them thoughtfully, fills the ladle and drinks as the men work.

Curtain.

Scene 3

13th Day. Afternoon. Scene same as previous one.

(The difference is the absence of the pestle, the mortar, baskets, trays and grains. Chapwanya is squatting at the grave and tiding it. Nyamaropa is pensively seated on a low stool, stroking his beard.)

Nyamaropa

I've heard you, Chapwanya. I'm not a frog; so I won't plunge. I need time to consider.

Chapwanya

(Harrowing pebbles on the grave)

Until I know where you stand I must regard you with suspicion. The others who were here yesterday had time to consider, too. They're in their homesteads pondering whether to await obliteration or take it to the Amandabili.

Nyamaropa

This is a weighty matter yelling for statesmanship. My mind is made up; deciding tomorrow might be one day too late.

Chapwanya

(Looks up at him and rises after a while. Crosses to him and shakes his hand)

Manliness and instant decisiveness are synonymous. The mongoose kills the cobra because the serpent always hesitates to strike.

Nyamaropa

But what did you see in me?

Chapwanya

(Holding on to his hand)

Your youthful independence and innovation, your vast pool of bitter battle experience, and your persuasive skills hardened by years of emissary obligations.

Nyamaropa rises, touched.

Today heroes are seen as unbranded stray cattle, Nyamaropa. In you is also the genius that remembers events, wars and all our important dates. I'm proud to say I saw kings and clansmen of standing consult your genius. A man of knowledge is an asset to any state.

Nyamaropa

But Changamire had knowledge, yet clansmen now despise it.

Chapwanya

A mastering of foreign myths, foreign legends and foreign divinities isn't knowledge. Unlike him, you're grounded in our ethnicity and avowed to the preservation of our history. Flattery isn't my province, but you're a living testament of our heritage.

Nyamaropa

Thank you, Chapwanya. In recent years I saw myself as hoary and past my brilliance. You've added more years to my life. However, it isn't knowledge of our customs that will rekindle Rozvi pride, but the spear aided by who ever can manipulate mediums.

Chapwanya

It is such knowledge that will drive the restoration. In your opinion how should we proceed?

Nyamaropa

The poor must be blindfolded first, for their ultimate benefit. Poor clansmen suffer from this peculiar disease which makes them vulnerability; their desire to please the wealthy. We'll have to exploit their voice.

Chapwany nods in appreciation and lets go of Nyamaropa's hand. Both sit. If you aim to sit on that throne you don't have my support. Kingship that changes houses altogether causes civil war. You come from a lineage of pastoralists and hunters.

Chapwanya

But the Amandabili are flourishing on our pastures. They looted our Zebu and longhorn cattle, and left us scraggy beasts ever hobbling to their deaths with disease. I tried to turn to hunting, but the marginalisation we endure for the benefit of the foreign hunters is unbearable. Now it's worse. Ivory hunting would earn me a thorough beating courtesy of Dombo's concessions.

Nyamaropa

You're a wounded buffalo. A traumatic buffalo tears down whatever lies in its path. It takes no precaution and trudges to its death as a result. Personally I wouldn't want a terribly bitter man on that throne; he would lack rationality. If Dombo can't be king then his immediate young brother will be. He is one of six brothers from the same parentage. From the frivolous Dombo down to the sixth brother, public opinion and diviners ought to come up with a common name for the appointment. The diviners have the last say, but normally a popular candidate without spiritual or societal blemish is appointed. For all the six of them to fail would be unprecedented.

Chapwanya
But the six have a voracious appetite for foreign languages and customs. Theirs is a shameful arabic brotherhood.

Nyamaropa
The folly of the brothers stands in my eyes. They greet one another in Turkish, Hindu or Portuguese. The youngest had an impromptu circumcision at the hands of a Swahili trader during a beer drinking binge.

Chapwanya
The kingship must skip all of these imbeciles. This campaign shall not be without grave risks.

Nyamaropa
A few deaths we can bear, but a full-fledged civil war is devastating.

Chapwanya
I need you, Nyamaropa, so that we avert such a disaster.

Nyamaropa
What if the three elders you spoke to recoil and turn traitors?

Chapwanya
I've always prevailed on them. Besides, nothing halts the rising of the sun. Aided or not, I'll bar the horse-rider from the throne.

Nyamaropa
About your discontent with Dombo you spoke plainly. But about your preferred candidate you're mum. Perhaps I should leave you alone to your dreams.

Chapwanya
The blood of pastoralists and hunters forbids me to sit on that throne. In the same house the kingship shall remain, but we'll make it skip a generation. A young, impressionable man will lead the Rozvi. His ears are still virgin to the satanic Amandabili battle-cry. Royal blood flows in his veins. He'll sit on that throne and represent our interest, yours and mine. Accordingly, we'll advise and reign under him as Provincial Chiefs.

Nyamaropa
meantime we must prepare for war.

Chapwanya

It might cause a stir and a fracas but not war. The crown shall land on Gungwa's head.

Nyamaropa

(*Rises abruptly in disbelief*)

Gungwa, you said!

Chapwanya

You heard me well...Gungwa, Zunzanyika's eldest son.
Nyamaropa shakes his head in a thoughtful stupor.

Nyamaropa

Gungwa is unmarried and barely eighteen. It's not confounding that his seed is still geese on water. The boy has never seen war. There's no assurance he will be able to stand the sight of blood. And you expect this boy to spearhead our campaign against the demonic Amandabili? Tell me this is an elaborate joke, Chapwanya.

Chapwanya

His incapabilities and youthfulness are his merits in this scheme. Thinkers can do wonders with an impressionable young man wielding power. All a leader requires are sound advisors, not fertility or a goatee beard. Now are you in or out?

Nyamaropa

(*Sits and holds his temples*)

This route shall be fraught with danger and bloodbaths. The arabic brotherhood will rise against us. We'll be killed and our wealth plundered. I had agreed in principle, but now I ask for time to consider.

Chapwanya

That luxury you won't enjoy because you now know too much. Are you in or out, Nyamaropa, I demand to know?
Suddenly from off-stage booms the neighing and galloping of a horse. The two men rise and strain to see off-stage, i.e. between gaps in the stockade and tree trunks. The neighing and the galloping noises rise and fade almost instantly.
There goes your self-appointed king. See how he displays his idiocy.

Nyamaropa

Let him dream on, Chapwanya. They say it's dangerous to wake a sleepwalker while he's at it. (*Suddenly recalls something*) Sit down. If this hasn't yet reached your ears it might halt your heart.
Both sit, Chapwanya's eyes inquisitively on him.

The decree that barred the white-skins from visiting the village was overturned. The preacher and the woman were brought to the village yesterday at sunset.

Chapwanya
(Lamentably)

Will good news ever console my ears? Tell me in detail what happened.

Nyamaropa

Yesterday at noon Dombo rode to the wooden house. He stayed very long in the house. Outside, the two baVenda brutes stood guard, long guns at the ready as usual. After a long while, Dombo and Mapfupa came out and spoke to the baVenda. I saw it all; when one is at my homestead one sees all that goes on at the house.

Chapwanya

So this alias has stuck to him like a limpet?

Nyamaropa

Yes, everyone now calls him by no other name except Mapfupa. A stranger can be forgiven for thinking clansmen are conversing about a Rozvi on hearing them mention the name with zeal.

Chapwanya

It seems this land lost the ability to produce heroes and must import them. Go on, Nyamaropa.

Nyamaropa

The baVenda mounted horses and rode out eastwards. Dombo rode westwards. Moments later the ever-armed Mapfupa casually rode northwards towing a saddled horse. Considerable time passed without any of them returning. It was moments before sunset when they all rode back as one party from the direction of Chikasha Forest.

Chapwanya

Is that when they brought the preacher and the woman?

Nyamaropa

Yes. *(With mimic gestures and actions)* One baVenda man rode ahead, leading the horse with one hand and wielding a poised gun with the other. The other brute brought up the rear, vigilant and fierce. Dombo and Mapfupa rode on the flanks of the path – between them the preacher and the woman on the same horseback. The party raised dust as it sped on full gallop, women dashing out of the way and breaking their water gourds, some almost losing limbs. Those who witnessed them rumbling in thought Ibwe was being invaded. Against a sinking sun, the silhouette was just deathly. If someone in the party had sounded a war-cry Ibwe would've been taken without them firing a single shot.

Chapwanya's countenance falls and becomes mournful. Nyamaropa shakes his head, but, devoid of consolation, continues with the narration.

The galloping bolt of lightning was soon at the wooden house. The white-skins and Dombo vanished into the house, but the baVenda didn't dismount. They took to perambulating the periphery of the premises, and everything was quiet. But from where they came the dust was yet to settle.

Chapwanya
The white-skins from Chikasha Forest should have been bludgeoned on sight.

Nyamaropa
Who would've dared! Mapfupa was an effigy of death. The baVenda brutes were as efferous as suckling leopards.

Chapwanya
(Annoyed)
At times solitude and stigma are valuable tools against such depressing narratives.

Nyamaropa
(Continuing)
In the villages the news spread. Clansmen came out of their homesteads and watched the wooden house from a distance. But there seemed to be a fatal attraction.

Chapwanya
Are you going to tell me clansmen were killed yesterday?

Nyamaropa
On the contrary, they were pampered with words akin to a seduction. Clansmen edged towards the house, possibly to spy and satisfy curiosity, or better still, to execute the white-skins for breaching the decree. About twenty armed men got there ahead of everybody. Dombo emerged from the house and spoke to them briefly, the baVenda brutes keeping a wary eye on the group. Wild gestures from the group were indicative of an argument, but Dombo prevailed on them. Soon I saw Dombo retreating to

stand on the veranda while the group sat down in the cleared open acreage in front of the house. People watching from a safe distance were overtaken by curiosity and converged at the house. I joined them. Every space was taken up. Clansmen looked forward to the execution of the aliens with a passion.

Chapwanya

A decree has been veritably breached. Executions were proper.

Nyamaropa

The gathering affirmed that executions were moments away. Three necks, including Dombo's, were to be broken.

Chapwanya

Your story lacks a happy ending because a while ago we saw Dombo. Did the aliens meet their fate then?

Nyamaropa

You asked for details and I'm furnishing you with them. Overwhelmed by numbers, the baVenda dismounted and stood guard at the entrance of the house, their guns aimed into the crowd. The gathering began to scuffle as loudly it vied for blood, but caution calmed the people aware that in such a crowd one bullet could bring down several. The gathering quietened and sat itself down. But near the house the hangman and his two assistants were already setting up the scaffold. In no time the accursed structure towered above everybody, its four nooses dangling in the wind. The scaffold evoked grim memories of hapless clansmen who perished over petty issues. On account of that, silence descended on the gathering.

Chapwanya

This is far from a heroic story. Spare me the details now.

Nyamaropa

Well, the reverend came out, followed by the ever-armed Mapfupa, then the woman, wide-eyed and visibly shaking. She clung to eagle-eyed Mapfupa whose movements were deliberately slow and dangerously cautious. The baVenda brutes crouched on their knees guns aimed at the gathering. Had someone uttered a battle-cry a massacre would have ensued.

Chapwanya

Which group would've succumbed?

Nyamaropa

It was the clansmen who would've borne the brunt of death.
Many of us would've fallen though in the end we would've killed
them all.

Chapwanya

Your exaltation of the enemy irritates me, Nyamaropa. I thought
you'd reflect the noblest desires of this land. You should've led
the attack.

Nyamaropa

There was no need, the scaffold was ready and waiting, besides
I'm now old and slow. No force was used. The teacher went up
the ladder of the scaffold and stood on the platform. The hangman
followed him up. But one of the trap-doors malfunctioned and
the hangman fell through, breaking his leg. A scrounging for a
substitute hangman ensued.

Chapwanya

But the assistants should've got on with the job.

Nyamaropa

Cautious clansmen are always wary of consequences. A freak
offered to perform the execution, but asked to gulp a gourd of
beer first. While some clansmen rushed about for the beer, the
white-skin opened his mouth to speak his final words. Everyone
saw and heard him; that scaffold is taller than a giraffe. His
sangfroid voice, borne by an invisible fire, rose to a crescendo.

Chapwanya

You're singing in praise of the enemy, Nyamaropa.

Nyamaropa

I'm neither adding nor subtracting. (*Continuing*) He narrated the
saddest of stories. He spoke about three trees on a hill. On two
of the trees hang two thieves. On the middle one dangles a
condemned innocent man. And there the speaker was, on the
platform of death, condemned but not pleading for his life. Instead
he was whole-heartedly asking the Rozvi to accept the spirit of
his crucified god, a dead man. He was oblivious to the four nooses
brushing his hair as he paced on the platform. Below him a sea of
eyes followed his movements until he was a silhouette. But the
fire in his voice didn't fade. That white-skin is a spirit.

Chapwanya
Tell me about the volunteer hangman, perhaps I can find a smile for my face.

Nyamaropa
Oh! (*Laughs coyly*) By the time the freak was drunk and scuffling towards the scaffold, hoards of clansmen, mostly women, were clamouring for the teacher to initiate them into his faith.

Chapwanya
Most baffling! But a decree had been broken, apparently.

Nyamaropa
Division saved the white-skins. At the end only pockets of clansmen wanted him hanged. Their voices were pathetically drowned by the deafening ones of their frenzied opposition. Repentant voices shouted that the matter required the attention of the Council of Elders. Some warned it was an ill-omen to hang anyone while the king ailed gravely. The murderous few shoved and cursed, a melee was taking root. The hoards drove the freak and his faction away.

Chapwanya
(*Dismayed, rises and walks to the furthest point. He turns and faces him*)
This isn't the Nyamaropa who vowed to perish in battle.
(*Waving dismissively at him*) Go home, spent warrior.
Nyamaropa rises demurs and waves back. He starts towards the exit in the opposite direction, but stops and turns.

Nyamaropa
His name is Holbrook or Reverend or Pastor. The lady's name is Shannon.
An uneasy brief silence ensues.

Chapwanya
(*Frowns and waves again*)
You're tired. Go home, Nyamaropa. You asked for time to consider; you've got it. Soon I shall beat the drum. If you're interested come, if in doubt stay at home I won't begrudge you. You can also convert and bow to the new gods.
Exit Nyamaropa leaving Chapwanya staring.

Curtain.

Act III

Scene 1

14th Day. Night. Inside Gungwa's circular sleeping-hut.

(The wall is built of poles and clay, and on it hangs five large and magnificent framed portraits, all hand-drawn. The one closest to the door depicts a merchant caravan; the second, Egyptian Pyramids; the third, an unknown sultan in a fez; the fourth, a sailing steamer; and the fifth, a trade-route map depicting Africa, the Middle East and lower parts of Europe and Asia.

There's an imported folding chair, an ethnic stool and an old exotic table on which are arranged two ceramic jars, a cup, a propped up hand-mirror, and a sheathed dagger. Under the table are three pairs of sandals and a stack of neatly folded cloths. Near the table is a small wooden crate, about half a cubic metre. Two kerosene lamps illuminate the room, one on the table, the other near the head of a restless Gungwa lying on hides in the centre of the room. In only a loincloth, he turns and groans in his sleep.

In the room, on the floor and isolated, are items on a reed mat entirely covered by a printed mediumistic cloth; about a square metre of a large red piece of fabric splashed with neatly placed white dots intermingling with arrowhead-like black designs. Two unlit candle sticks flank the covered items on the floor. Gungwa suddenly cries out, jerks and sits up, draws his knees up and rests his elbows on them, his countenance nightmarish, his chest heaving. He looks about, fixes his eyes on the covered items, and then crawls to the wooden crate from which he takes out a box of matches. Rising, he yawns and stares at the covered items. He crosses to them, stoops and lights the candle sticks, and kneels down.)

Gungwa
(Hands clasped in supplication)

Spirit-elders, I'm but a boy who knows not how to pray.
Of birth noble I am, but my ignorance is a manmade sway.
Why am I in darkness as if guilty of an ignominy?
In ceaseless spasms of throbbing agony
Far-reaching thorns, jiggered, hurt my heart.
This is my father's shrine, which I borrowed from his hut
Gingerly, he removes the mediumistic cloth and drapes it on his shoulder. Uncovered is a personal shrine on the reed mat; a gourd, a wooden plate, a snuff calabash, a walking stick, a battle-axe, and two small lengths of black and white cloth folded neatly.

Enter Dombo quietly and stands near the door. The cloth covering his upper and lower body is striking. In sandaled feet and wrists covered with bangles he wears a holstered handgun around his waist and has an eye-catching necklace. Dombo folds his arms across his chest and watches. Gungwa backs Dombo unaware of his presence.
(Clapping hands gently):

> Ancestors, in unknown places the lion has slept.
> When I last saw him, out of his body health had leapt
> In private or in public no clansman dares say a word.
> Oblique the mystery remains until you say a word.
> O, I dream dreams, of my father's face hide-covered.
> Behind the hide, is he smiling, frowning or haggard?
> Like an apparition he rises from the depths, conjuring dread.
> Is the Rozvi fascination gravely ailing or dead?

Dombo claps hands in mock applause and startles Gungwa. He turns and rises. Dombo continues to clap his hands, smiling.

Gungwa

You startled me, uncle. I thought it was my father.

Dombo

(Stops clapping)

Always latch the door when you need privacy. (*Points at the shrine*) What's an adolescent doing with a shrine, Gungwa?

Gungwa

I must know where my father is.

Dombo

Play with your father's shrine and you'll cause his death and have yourself to blame. At your age you cannot know how to pray. A prince you are; poetry isn't meant for your mouth but your ears. You should have come to me.

Gungwa

Ever galloping on horseback, how could I have caught up with you? Go to any village, clansmen are using the most damning epithets to describe you.

Dombo

(Unruffled)

Be mindful all the time of your princely position. Reason of state doesn't guide the commoner's mind though the commoner isn't immune to considerations of power. To canoe criticism it takes two; one to speak and the other to hear. Avoid ordinary folk, or you risk doing damage to your person.

Dombo crosses to the folding chair and sits down. Gungwa remains standing beside the shrine.

Gungwa

Uncle, spare me these platitudes. Where's my father?

Dombo

Sit down, Gungwa, or do you challenge my seniority.

Gungwa

(Defiant)

I've had to endure the indecency of stealing my father's shrine. I've had to inquire from village elders because it appears there's a communal conspiracy to leave me in the dark. My own father's young brother won't tell me anything. Tomorrow I'm visiting vaChapwanya, he might know something.

Dombo

What does that rebel and dreamer know? Why would a prince mention that garrulous off-scouring of humanity?

Gungwa

My father holds him in high esteem, why do you rebuke him so?

Dombo

He is a rabid rebel, a madman of great proportion. I have always feared that at his invitation final calamity would pay the Rozvi a visit.

Gungwa

You still haven't told me why you deem him a rebel.

Dombo

Chapwanya rebelled against tradition. The evidence stares at him daily in his backyard... a grave. And by denouncing the Council of Elders he rebelled against your father, too.

Gungwa

But, uncle, if a man gluttonous, rebellious or cannibalistic were to point to me where my father is, would I lose anything?

Dombo

Your father ailed critically when you last saw him. He being a man of stature, of paramount essence and of unmatched wisdom, his condition persuaded us to seek unsurpassable treatment for him. To the land of our cousins, the Ndau, we rushed him. A renowned medicine-man is restoring him.

Gungwa crosses to another position, thoughtfully.

Gungwa

Supposing what you say is true, why then are you riding maniacally without rest? Customarily, you ought to be by my father's side rendering him brotherly affection. I regret to say, but the land is awash with bitter complaints about your decadence. You've thrown yourself headlong in front of criticism.

Dombo

The medicine-man prescribed something almost akin to solitude for him. The word of a medicine-man is like a decree.

Gungwa

(Sits on the low stool)

Rumour has it that he is dead.

Dombo lets out an eerie shriek then laughs. Annoyed, Gungwa grabs the mediumistic cloth draped on his shoulder and slams it on the floor in anger. Dombo reaches out and firmly holds Gungwa's hand, who tries in vain to free himself, momentarily giving up.

Dombo

(Toying with Gungwa's hand)

If he were dead you'd have been the first one to learn of it, my dear nephew. Illness had overtaken him when we took him out of the royal compound. For that reason the rumour of his passage didn't require strenuous creativity. If he were dead your head would've been shaven. This compound would've been packed with mourners as we speak, and every village head, counsellor and chief would've been summoned. *(Pause)* If you insist he is dead kindly furnish me with his remains that I may bury my brother.

Gungwa

The onus is on you, uncle; you took him away together with my mother and three of his senior wives. By being elusive, it's your own integrity you're forfeiting, uncle. *(Frees his hand)*

Dombo

Does forfeiture of my integrity describe my meteoric rise? My goals are noble, my craftsmanship stately and unselfish. I'll put to shame my disillusioned detractors. Instead of commoners complaining about how fate has disadvantaged them, they waste valuable time puzzling out a clear-cut succession.

Gungwa

Take no offence, uncle, but, one: Clansmen rebuke you for craving public attention like a child. Number two: You gave away ancestral land. Three: You're heartlessly extorting ivory from clansmen. The fourth: Non-ceremonial assumption of power.

Gungwa for a while holds out four fingers. Dombo rises. For a moment he paces quietly, like one at a loss.

Dombo
(Pacing)

Mapfupa brought in nine thoroughbreds, which I exercise thoroughly, or they'd die from sudden muscle laxity. Daily I ride each of the horses. If someone else were to do it they would steal our prestige. *(Halts. Counting off his fingers)* He gave us all the nine horses, the four-roomed house and all the furniture in it, and the two wagons. Everything is ours. Mapfupa is a wealthy hunter and wanderer.

Gungwa

Why is he still staying in the house and keeping the horses?

Dombo

My brother is ill, which makes me very sad, but I'm happy I'm acting in his best interest. Upon his return he shall honour me with many honours for the maintenance of order and the acquisitions. The baVenda are an important convenience. Massaging clansmen doesn't get orders carried out, but a small measure of heavy-handedness is needed. *(Points at the portrait of pyramids)* That's what built the pyramids and the castles of the great empires overseas. The *mfecane* wasn't the off-spring of an epic romance between Tshaka and his neighbours.

Gungwa

I'm astounded you see brutality as a means to an end.

Dombo

It's not brutality but a principle.

Gungwa

When is Mapfupa leaving?

Dombo

At the end of the season, according to our agreement. We'll take stock of our ivory to see if we shared it equally. He'll haul his share to the Limpopo River under the escort of our warriors.

Only Mapfupa, his share of ivory and the baVenda men shall cross the river. Across the Limpopo he has resourceful friends who'll ferry his freight to the coast.

Gungwa

Tell me about the *mfecane*. Clansmen speak about it in hushed tones.

Dombo

I regret talking about that great strife in Zululand over forty-five years ago. I was a toddler then. Our fathers suffered terrible losses. Over six groups of Sotho and Nguni-speaking people crossed the Limpopo from the south into Urozviland. All were fleeing the long arm of roaring Tshaka. All they sought was a passage to distant lands far from Tshaka, but they pillaged our land. I'll tell you more when you're older.

Dombo shakes his head ruefully and goes to sit on the chair.

With my share of the ivory I'll acquire guns and more horses, for swift mobility and efficiency in battle. The day before yesterday, courtesy of horses and guns, we charged like rampaging buffaloes from Chikasha Forest and brought in the reverend and his aide. No one could dare stand in our way.

Gungwa

Guns are cowardly. No heroism lies in aiming a gun at a distant valiant warrior and wasting him. Your aspirations will bring to an end honours for bravery on the battlefield. Surely, uncle, what tales of exploits could a gun-totting warrior tell on returning from war?

Dombo

With bullets we'll flush the Amandabili out of Guruuswa.

Gungwa

But by bringing back the barred aliens you breached a decree. Three bodies were meant to hang on that scaffold – the third one being yours.

Dombo

Three bodies were hanged on that scaffold. Had you been there you could've seen them.

Gungwa

I was in the crowd. No one was hanged.

Dombo

Three bodies did hang. Oration is a route out of a predicament; Holbrook demonstrated it exceptionally. The sun sinking behind

71

him, he took advantage and spoke himself into oblivion, a great distracting spell, until he was a silhouette. He continued to bellow until the silhouette blended with the darkness. Like a conundrum, he kept at it until light allegorically came out of the darkness.

Gungwa

No such thing happened, uncle. Please spare me falsehoods.

Dombo

I speak metaphorically. What took place was too figurative to be explained plainly. On that accursed scaffold darkness engulfed him. The clansmen couldn't see him anymore, but in their minds they saw the three trees and the three condemned men he preached about. The portrait he painted was so vivid and graphic that women were reduced to tears. His oratory skills and detachment from self swayed the clansmen. Instead of pleading for his life he took the opportunity to enlighten us about his gods. The Rozvi admired him for it; hence they stayed the execution. (*Rises, picks the kerosene lamp from the table and slowly moves around the hut, viewing the portraits as he speaks while holding out the light to them*) I didn't violate the decree. It remains standing, inexorable and solemn. I do admit I raised suspicion by bringing in the couple. But suspicion and the breaching of a decree are different things.

Gungwa

Your actions were irresponsible.

Dombo

The diviners should've stayed to enforce their decree. I don't represent these seers in any way, neither are my views or actions representative of them. On the contrary, I brought the couple in hoping that they would be killed on sight. We must reclaim Chikasha by getting rid of them one way or the other. (*Pauses at the last portrait. Staring at the portrait*) Tell me something, Gungwa.

Gungwa

What do you want to know, uncle?
Gungwa rises and yawns, stretching, and sits in the chair. Dombo remains paused at the portrait

Dombo

If hordes had dragged me up that scaffold, would you have charged at them in my defence?

Gungwa

Frankly, I would've turned my back and walked away.

Dombo

Your being my brother's son makes you my child. (*Turns and looks at him*) See me in the light of a father. Suspicion and mistrust ruin dynasties. Taking league with my detractors is self-condemnation. My plans are foolhardy. You can be a part of them.

He returns the lamp to the table and sits on the low stool from which he has to look up at Gungwa on the chair.

Gungwa

Mapfupa might vanish with all the ivory.

Dombo

The hunter's deep love for the couple is his frailty.

Gungwa

(*Matter-of-factly*)

Of course they should've some affection for one another; they hail from the same territory, speak the same language and pray to the same gods. And the three of them are far from home.

Dombo

The couple is the collateral. If Mapfupa breaches the terms or vanishes, the couple hangs.

Gungwa

Holbrook is a man of juju. I swear no one can kill him. Your hand would tremble. The hangman broke his leg.

Dombo

Should cause arise I would. On sound or broken legs I would stand and kill him. I'd even hang him twice for the fun of it. (*Realising an anomaly*) Why do you spit at custom, Gungwa? You can't sit on a high chair while I squat on a low stool.

Dombo rises and curtly gestures at Gungwa to rise from the chair. Gungwa rises reluctantly. Dombo nods. They exchange positions and sit.

Gungwa

(*Dismissively*)

It's nearly midnight. I must sleep.

Dombo

We're the nobility of this land, made of an essence different from commoners. Notions of honour, of one day ascending the throne, should permeate your mind.

Gungwa

You can't have come to tell me such things at this time of the night.

Dombo

State affairs consume much of my daytime. I came to honour you.

He unties a large knot on the flap of his lower cloth, revealing a handful of cowry shells mingled with coins. He holds the currency in his hands and begins to pour it from one hand into the other, continually, some shells and coins falling.

I brought you money to spend on yourself. Lately you've been wearing sorrow like a medal. Clansmen were beginning to whisper obscenities against me because of the dejection in your eyes. Don't be sad; your parents are alive. Perhaps it is idleness that has made you inquisitive. Tallying my ivory stock on a daily basis would be an ideal occupation. Once you're constantly by my side no malicious mouth will come to whisper things to you. (*Offering him the money*) Here, take it.

Gungwa stares at the money.

Take it, Gungwa. This is your uncle spoiling you a little.

Gungwa continues to stare at the money.

(*Firmly*) Take it, my son, your father gives it to you in good faith. I'm not returning with this money. Whatever you need you shall get from me. It ought to be beneath you to approach commoners for anything.

A tense silence. Dombo forcibly places the money in Gungwa's hands and rises. Gungwa appraises the coins briefly, looks up at his uncle and rises, too.

Gungwa

(*Furiously*)

You aren't my father! My father is dead!

Frowning, Gungwa throws all the coins and the cowry shells at Dombo's feet.

Dombo

(*Outraged*)

You're very foolish, Gungwa! You've a lot of growing up to do! Chances are you aren't my brother's son after all… perhaps a shoddy stepson, a spiteful bastard! (*Poking a finger on Dombo's brow*) I can declare you my enemy. On principle I pulverise my enemies.

Gungwa

I've nothing to consider, uncle. Tomorrow I'll start searching for my father's body. (*Points at the door*) Can I sleep now?

Dombo looks at the money on the floor, makes a pitying gesture at Gungwa, turns and walks towards the door. At the door Dombo pauses and turns. He shakes his head and makes another pitying gesture at Gungwa. Exit Dombo.

Curtain.

Scene 2

15th Day. Daybreak. Chapwanya's unkempt homestead backyard.

(Lying about are the low wooden stools and the drum, among other paraphernalia. Chapwanya's battle-axe is on the grave. Chapwanya is alone and making a single-fowl bird-cage using twigs and straps of bark. The cage is almost complete. An off-stage staccato drumbeat jerks him from a reverie. He corks an ear to his left, but the drumbeat dies. Her shakes his head and begins to whistle as he resumes making the cage. Moments later another drumbeat, this one lugubriously slow, comes from the same source. He freezes and inclines his head, disturbed. The drumbeat continues. He sets the cage down, rises and starts to the left, but the drumbeat stops. As he stares in the direction the drumbeat came from, the staccato drumbeat comes again, baffling him. Shaking his head, he continues to the edge of the yard where he strains to see in the distance seemingly over the stockade. The drumbeat ceases. Perplexed, he returns to his stool and sits idly in reflection. But the sombre drumbeat sounds again from the same source.
Enter Nyamaropa briskly. He picks a stool and sits near Chapwanya.)

Nyamaropa

You heard the bewildering drumbeats? The first summoned the elders. The second was mystifying, somewhat like a dirge. Could someone have decided to announce Changamire's death?
The drumbeats come again, alternating between brief pauses, then fall silent.

Chapwanya

The convening of the Council is clear. But the second drumbeat remains a funereal enigma. Beware of the horse-rider's gimmicks. One of us must go and hear his rhapsody, or events on the ground might overtake us.

Nyamaropa

An adversary with a penchant for accosting clansmen might say one word too many.

Chapwanya

I beseech you, Nyamaropa, to attend the meeting. Your attendance won't be ghostly; you didn't denounce the Council. I cannot sit on a council I denigrated. This second meeting of ours will proceed, but go and be the opposition's ear. Take your leave immediately;

the drumbeat had urgency in it.

Exit Nyamaropa hurriedly. The drumbeats sound again, alternatively. Enter Chinake and Gundu. The drumming stops.

Gundu
(On appearing, to Chapwanya)

The sorrowful drumbeat... we can't place it. It seems foreign hands have taken over our signals.

The three sit in meditative silence.

Chapwanya

Nyamaropa was here, and left for the elders' meeting. He'll inform us accordingly. Our absence at the meeting will get into their eyes.

Chinake

Instinct tells me we start mourning Changamire today. The calamitous two years of mourning have begun.

Gundu

Brother shall slay brother. We ought to act with haste before a *tumbare* is appointed to run the state.

Chapwanya

Dombo could forgo such courtesy and ascend the throne. Bending to custom has never been his preserve. I doubt if he has the patience to let someone hold the reigns for two solid years.

Gundu

The diviners haven't returned. How is Zunzanyika going to be mourned and buried?

Chinake

Perhaps Dombo has opted for a ritual-free burial, one not even befitting the burial of a child. The desire for power can make him bury his brother like a carcass. *(Picks the bird-cage and appraises it)* You intend to send a fowl to a far away relation?

Chapwanya

Today we inform Gungwa of the responsibility he'll assume. A goat for a token was my preference, but then it would be too conspicuous. A cock will have to do. Nyamaropa will take the cock to him tonight and rein him in before thoughts of suicide wrest him from us. If the boy accepts the token then we'll can rest assured he's in our fold.

Enter Makeredza bearing a gourd of frothing beer. Gundu rises and gladly goes to relieve him of the gourd, which he sets before all of them as Makeredza finds a stool and sits.

76

Chapwanya
(Clapping hands in appreciation)
Welcome, Makeredza, but why did you overburden yourself by bringing us a brew?

Makeredza
I'm returning a favour. Let us be jovial as we lay the foundations for the kingdom's restoration.

Gundu
(Clapping mildly)
Thank you, Makeredza. How's your family this morning?

Makeredza
The children chatter, their mothers busy themselves with chores. Did you hear the drumbeats?

Chinake
We heard them, though the second one was mysterious.

Makeredza
I'm remotely familiar with it. It could be a redemptive drumbeat that normally heralds a major state funeral. It has something to do with appeasement, if hawks haven't pecked at my memory.

Gundu
Then it might mean a medium has come out of hiding. But Nyamaropa will put us in the light. Meanwhile send anxiety on an errand or it will strangle us. We came to strategise and to hear the ultimate benefits.

Chapwanya
You'll excuse me momentarily, elders. *(Rises and exits)*

Chinake
(Whispering)
Elders, do we fully understand what we're getting into or we've been hoodwinked against our will? I'm not sure if I should take league with him. Actually, my mind isn't fully made up, yet I find myself coming here again.

Gundu
My mind is made up. Chapwanya has that singular quality which makes an honest man. A man who talks very fast has no time to listen to himself. Shoddy men speak slowly and are painfully verbose. Chapwanya is an honest, laconic fast-talker. It's a pity he isn't eyeing the throne himself.

Chinake

What's your understanding of this man, Makeredza?

Makeredza

What comes first to this man is the land, which is why he wasn't exactly bothered when his family deserted him. For this land he could lie on a bed of cacti. Such clansmen are rare and deserve a following.

Gundu

Such people merit a following, like Holbrook's Christ who laid down his life for his cause.

Chinake

Please spare us talk of Holbrook and his Christ.

Gundu

Holbrook hasn't left Ibwe ever since the evening of the sermon on the scaffold. (*Sadly*) Scores of clansmen are converting. The hangman converted that very evening. Fanatics are leaving this morning for Chikasha Forest to assist in the construction of a settlement in that abominable wilderness. It's inconceivable, to say the least. Some clansmen have already given Holbrook ivory and gold nuggets. Some brought him cattle and goats.

Makeredza

It's a devil of a practice by poor men and women!

Chinake

But what incentives do the Rozvi see in foreign gods?

Gundu

Holbrook says his god is all-powerful. Most people are doing it to protect themselves from Chemusango and the unuttered threat of an Amandabili raid. I gather in a few days Holbrook is taking the converts to Runde River to immense his idiots in our holy river. We must stop him.

Chinake

Man of flesh cannot wage a war on behalf of spirits. Encourage them to go to the river. *Njuzu*, the resident goddess of the river, awaits them. Vengeance is hers.

Enter Chapwanya carrying four exotic ceramic mugs. He sets the mugs near the gourd and sits.

Chapwanya

Drink from these charms notables of this land.

Gundu claps his hands and immediately fills all the mugs. Soon everyone is sipping and nursing his own mug.

I thank you for coming. This is the plan: Tonight a veteran of coercion will prevail on Gungwa. We'll find him five virgins of impeccable character and flawless beauty to marry. This will bolster his stature. But due to the curative rulership of a *tumbare*, the royal herd won't be accessible to Gungwa for that purpose. We'll have to draw the cattle from ours. Are there any objections?

Chinake
Can we be assured of the recovery of our wealth?

Chapwanya
This is a venture, be informed accordingly, Chinake. (*Continuing*) The second phase is to get him into exile for his security. The third phase is the gist of our engagement, the campaign for his acceptance. By affluence and influence we'll convince the Rozvi.

Makeredza
We preach Gungwa to everybody from Provincial Chiefs to ordinary clansmen. General Gwenhere is likely to be appointed *tumbare*. He is a friend of mine, a very equitable man. By refusing to hang cowardly clansmen he averted genocide. We can prevail upon him to hand power to Gungwa. He talks about Dombo with indignation. The army is already in our palms.

Gundu
I was doubtful, now I don't see anything that would hinder our boy.

Chapwanya
Should our diviners remain in hiding, we shall have to hire one outside our territory to appoint and install him. If we choose to be blatant we can start grooming bogus mediums now. Nothing stops his ascendancy.

Chinake
One way or the other the land ought to have diviners. Can we hear about the fruits?

Chapwanya
He shall appoint us Provincial Chiefs, and naturally we'll constitute the king's Advisory Council. Our army shall plunder the Amandabili, and we shall partake of the thousands of the enemy's cattle.

Makeredza
(Contemplatively)

Subduing Lo Bengula shall win us back the vassalage of the Kalanga, the Tonga and the Shangwe. We're talking insurmountable wealth here. May our plans enjoy the blessings of *Chikara* —Awe-inspirer.
Enter Nyamaropa clapping his hands. All look at him expectantly. He sits but the stares are compelling.

Nyamaropa

Dombo, backed by his five brothers, has finally announced Changamire's death. The whole story is an elaborate falsehood. Officially, he died in the hands of a Ndau medicine-man, and was quickly cremated. The medicine-man himself, a sardonic and threatening old man, is at the meeting. He'll preside over mourning and a ritualistic burial.

Chinake

He brought ashes?

Nyamaropa

He brought nothing but the story. In lieu of Changamire's remains they're going to entomb the head of a goat in a few days. No one dared contest the apparent lies. Dombo was restless, un-holstering and holstering the handgun as he sat. The baVenda brutes were present, so was Mapfupa. We were under siege. All we did was express our condolences.
Nyamaropa pauses and shakes his head pitiably, but the elders spur him on impatiently with gestures.

Then two breathless young men came to the meeting. They'd stumbled on the body of the embalmer on their way to Chikasha Forest. That quiet, solitary elder who never quarrelled with anybody is dead. The two young men directly reported their finding to the meeting to Dombo's annoyance. He dismissed them rather curtly.

Gundu

Did they say what he seemed to have died of?

Nyamaropa

They found the body in a kopje along the broad path that leads to Chikasha Forest. A wound akin to a battle-axe strike was said to be in the back of the embalmer's head. We flinched on hearing the description of the wound. But the royal brothers listened without emotion.

Makeredza

Have the king's wives returned then?

Nyamaropa

They're missing. The medicine-man said they left Ndauland ahead of him soon after the cremation. They vanished without trace between the two kingdoms, the four of them. Dombo was adamant they must have fallen prey to predators. The elders concurred weakly. Agonised, I just left the meeting unceremoniously.

Chinake

If only he hadn't ridden that horse the five of them would've been alive today. His insensitive joviality in a period of sorrow caught everyone's eye. He had to kill witnesses for his baloney of lies to hold. Now poor Gungwa has lost a mother.

Chapwanya

And it's now a conspiracy that involves aliens too.

Enter Gungwa clapping his hands, and almost crouching in humility. The elders exchange bemused glances. He wears two pieces of a similar cloth; one covering his lower body and the other the upper. He's in sandals and an eye-catching necklace, all foreign.

Chapwanya

O, royal blood, have you come to honour us with many honours?

Gungwa

(Approaching and still clapping)

O, select gathering of elders, hallowed is this day for me to find knowledge assembled. Befitting honours I'll bring when the object of my visit is achieved. (*Picks a stool and sits a respectful distance from the elders*) I come in peace and as a beggar of knowledge. (*Claps more loudly then stops*)

Nyamaropa

Knowledge is what we brood on, broach and broker ceaselessly.

Gungwa

With my eyes I saw you dish knowledge to my father. Of bountiful years your mouth speaks, and Rozvi ears savour their succulence. Of seasons of famine and tumult you prattle. But I don't seek abyssmal knowledge, of the birth of dynasties or the causes of famous ancient battles. I die to know where my father is. Settle my heart, elders, I beg you.

Chinake

Elders, of his own accord he seeks knowledge. With it come wisdom, an arousal and a renaissance. There can't be a future if the youth is kept askance in darkness.

Chapwanya

Nyamaropa, this is your domain. We'll leave you to it, and pray we have cause to celebrate on our return. (*To Gungwa*) What you wish to know under the circumstances assails the heart. May the assault bring vengeance, and may the vengeance be your uncustomary initiation into adulthood.

Chapwanya sets the gourd of beer and a mug directly before Nyamaropa. Exit everyone except Nyamaropa and Gungwa. Suddenly off-stage comes bouts of weeping and wailing, from all directions, shrilly and largely feminine. Gungwa is confounded and looks at Nyamaropa inquisitively.

Gungwa

Why is there such wailing so suddenly?

Nyamaropa

Brace yourself or you risk running amok (*Indifferently*) You have my condolences, son. Your father's death has been announced.
Gungwa is dumbfounded.
Official mourning has begun. Your mother and the three other wives were murdered, too. I'm sorry. Changamire was bewitched, but your mother was murdered, a victim of Dombo's atrocious selfishness. The same man is guilty of entombing your father without ceremony. There's a falsehood to conceal and an ambition to cherish. The cost is the blood of kith and kin.

Gungwa

(*Voice quivering*)

Is this a nightmare or what?

Nyamaropa

(*Calmly*)

No, this isn't what you think. I'm breaking the news of your parent's death to you, Gungwa. (*Emphatically*) They're dead, you won't see them anymore.

Gungwa falls from the stool and lies inert. Nyamaropa glances at him casually and fills the mug with beer. For a while he sips quietly and leisurely unmindful of the adolescent. After a lengthy while Gungwa coughs and comes to, sitting up. He looks blankly at the elder.

Welcome back, Gungwa. (*Non-committal*) I was telling you of the death of your parents. Accept it.

Gungwa ogles blankly at him and holds his head fleetingly. Off-stage the weeping and wailing comes again from all directions, rising, falling, then fading to a hum.
In an unknown cave somewhere lies your father's mummy, perhaps your mother's body, too. They lie in darkness without rites or honours, like unworthy carcasses.

Gungwa suddenly breaks down and weeps inconsolably. Nyamaropa sips nonchalantly, looking away. Shortly, Gungwa wipes his tears.

Gungwa
(*Sobbing and snivelling*)
The wailing confirms it. An elder of your reputation cannot dispense lies.

Nyamaropa
But your father was a thief and a coward.
Gungwa looks at him sharply, offended.
He laid claim to the throne in a daring scandal seven years ago.

Gungwa
That's absurd! He's dead, why do you slander a dead man? He took over from Sabambamu, his elder brother. Their father was Chirisamhuru.

Nyamaropa
So it seemed, son. Seven years ago the last undisputed heir, Changamire Sabambamu, was abducted by the Amandabili. They took him to Guruuswa and killed him, bringing to an end a dynasty. Confusion and feuding arose during the succession. But your father claimed the throne in a bloody campaign.

Gungwa
But my father was entitled to it by right and birth.

Nyamaropa
(*Looks away*)
Who was Zunzanyika? He was nephew to Changamire Sibambamu; being a son of Sibambamu's sister. But because your father was raised in the royal compound, and your father was close to the king, many believed Zunzanyika and Sibambamu were brothers. Years eroded knowledge of the proper relationship. The false brotherhood took prominence.

Gungwa
(*In protest*)

My parents are dead, yet you assail me with an irresponsible discourse! What's the meaning, vaNyamaropa?

Nyamaropa
(*Ignoring him*)

After the abduction your father claimed kingship. He was uncompromising; men and women fell. Your uncles stood by him. I can see the desire to shed blood hasn't left them ever since. Your father would've confided this in you upon your coming of age, but death is an untimely stalker.

Gungwa ponders and shakes his head, markedly hurt and sorrowful.

Gungwa

You mean Changamire Chirisamhuru wasn't my grandfather?

Nyamaropa

Rejoice you aren't related to him. About forty-five years ago during the *mfecane* a Nguni female warrior, by name Nyamazana, slew him at his court. Chirisamhuru's death remains an embarrassment to every Rozvi to this day.

Gungwa
(*Ruffling his hair*)

This is my worst nightmare. I want to leave and spare myself the brunt of your scalding brutal knowledge. But I can't because I don't know you to be cynical. I would require a devil of a heart to thank you, vaNyamaropa. But still I must rise above personal pain. I must see kindness out of dark words. (*Stops ruffling his hair*) Be ruthless with me now; I must know everything.

Nyamaropa

The last seven years saw your father forwarding ransom after ransom to Lo Bengula. Merchants ill-advised him thus; for peace to prevail and their trade to flourish.

Gungwa

But it spared lives. The objective was met.

Nyamaropa

Land and integrity aren't ransomable. Annually, a hundred Zebu and as many longhorns were purportedly loaned to the Kalanga. The Kalanga Chief kept them for a month then took them to Lo Bengula by night.

Gungwa

Perhaps he hoped to attack one day when the ransom would have put the enemy off-guard.

Nyamaropa

Seven years is a long period to demur an attack. Your father stuffed himself with unprofitable knowledge, parroted exotic folklores just to conceal his cowardice. If he hadn't exploited folkloric stories he probably would have frolicked naked for the same goal. (*Pause*) Go home and mourn your father. Soon they'll declare your mother dead and she shall be mourned in earnest. But as you mourn beware of the return of the diviners. They'll cast lots and dispossess you of your heritage. And beware of the defensive arrows from your uncles.

Gungwa

In the absence of diviners what to do eludes me. But this agonising mystery needs unravelling… a dénouement.

Nyamaropa

The divines are stranded between two savages. Maybe that's why they can't return. On the one hand, they must cast lots, which renders them the opposition in your uncles' eyes. And your uncles slaughter the opposition. On the other hand, they could return and opt for silence. But the silence would torment the spirit-elders. The diviner's demise would be quick and brutal as a deterrent.

Gungwa

If they cast lots, won't the spirits protect them?

Nyamaropa

Gods are known to turn their backs on their favourites. That's why lately there was that grim spectacle at *Mwari's* shrine. That's why Holbrook's Christ had to die.

Gungwa

Why then did the hermit install my father without divining the rightful ruler?

Nyamaropa

Through the hermit the gods are protesting against the thievery and our docility. (*Points at the grave*) Had we not been agitated this grave wouldn't have been misplaced to rouse us. We wouldn't have been talking. The happenings around us belong to a pattern, which is ruthlessly awakening us from abyssmal slumber.

Gungwa

I'm not a thief. I'll never sit on that throne. Doing so would be harrowingly immoral. Somewhere a deserving family and a ruler live in obscurity because of us. The seers should come and cast their lots.

Nyamaropa

A new king would use the spear to ascertain his security, to forever silence voices likely to bother him in the future. You and all your relations would be slaughtered.

Gungwa

(*Holding his head*)

Oh, you barricade my option! What do I do?

Nyamaropa

The path to self-imposed exile remains open. Or you could shrug off cowardice and do the honourable thing; ascend that throne ahead of your uncles. There's a fire to be rekindled, a state to be edified.

Gungwa

(*In emotional soliloquy*)

Exile is punitive obscurity and self-dejection. Yet ascendancy is a short footpath with garlands on either side, but gore and carnage lurk in the flowers. The thought of taking human life, I find dispiriting. But killing is inevitable in one's lifetime. Now I shudder to think I must consider silencing my uncles to occupy a burgled chair.

Nyamaropa

Carnage cannot be dissociated from men. From the vagaries of nature come natural disasters borne on carnage. From the spear of man comes carnage. What's there to ponder? Anyway, be like your father, Gungwa; a cunning coward. Trek into exile beyond the Zambezi River. Go and pauperise yourself among callous strangers. Should the worst confront the Rozvi, we'll rally behind Dombo. (*Pointing the exit*) Now go home and mourn your father. I've nothing further to expound to animated timidity.

Gungwa doesn't stir. Nyamaropa points fixedly at the exit.

Gungwa

(*Rises in fury*): Here the remains of my parents lie! Here my unsuspecting enemies frolic! Bravery isn't the white stork that migrates seasonally! (*Thrusts a hand towards the elder*) Find me a machete now, and I'll instantly bring you six heads!

Nyamaropa looks up at him in disbelief. Gungwa's fury mounts and he doesn't withdraw the demanding hand. Speechless, the elder rises, his eyes fixed at the adolescent seemingly set to pounce at him.

Nyamaropa

(Overjoyed. Looks skywards.)

O! *Mutangakugara* – Primordial Beginner, hearer of genuine prayers, with sincerity I thank you! Now I know that the exit out of these doldrums was ordained by you! (*Crosses over to Gungwa and takes the latter's hand in his*) Cut no throats, son. Go home and mourn with resignation. Vengeance is yours, but the execution thereof shall be by the hands of others. The elders you saw here are behind you. Welcome aboard, Gungwa.

The elder embraces an unbelieving Gungwa.

Curtain.

Scene 3

22ⁿᵈ Day. Noon. Dombo's homestead backyard.

(Dombo and Chikukwa are behind a hut in the extreme left of the background, i.e. upper-stage left. Dombo is receiving firing instructions from Chikukwa. The former on his knees aims a long-barrelled gun at an abstract human-size dummy of sticks and straw placed in the foreground diagonally from the position the two occupy, i.e. lower-stage right.

Dombo is in a conspicuous high turban, upper and lower body all expensive clothed in red. The holstered handgun is around his waist. Maasai-like white dots decorate his forehead and encircle his left eye. Exotic sandals and striking jewellery enhance his outlandish air. Chikukwa is barefoot and ordinarily dressed, a simple cloth covering his lower body.

In the foreground directly in front of them, i.e. lower-stage left, is a dinner table flanked by two chairs laid for two. A luncheon covered with saran wrap is on the table; bowls, dinner plates, inverted wine glasses, a bottle of wine, fruits and a jar of water, all foreign; and this setting is in sharp contrast to its surroundings.)

Dombo
(Aiming, Chikukwa helps steady his aim):
I'm glad the token burial went peacefully yesterday. But I heard whispers in that long procession. What bothered the clansmen?

Chikukwa
They want an investigation into Changamire's alleged medical treatment and cremation. The medicine-man's explanation was vague and irksome. Everyone prays for a speedy appointment of a military leader. The *tumbare* must oversee investigations and condemn possible murderers.

Dombo
I'm a man of equity, Chikukwa. Everything shall be investigated… the medicine-man, the medicine he used and its dosage, the actual cause of death…everything. Everyone's suspicion shall be quelled. Criminals shall be put to death; the scaffold is in perfect working order.

Chikukwa
(Standing behind him, verifying the aim)
At this point steady nerves are required, Sir. The target is now a sleeping baboon. Don't be distracted or lose focus. Hold your breath and brace yourself while your finger curls tightly around the trigger

until it discharges. Quickly reload, aim and fire again if you miss the target. Keep firing in quick succession until the target falls.

Dombo

(Rises and places the gun on his shoulder)

Your instructions summarise my immanent convictions in life. Upon them, naturally, I've founded personal principles that propel me to eminence. *(Turns and faces him. Parodying slowly)* Aim, focus and fire… fire repeatedly until the objective is achieved! The idea is to be maniacally goal-oriented in your endeavours.

Dombo suddenly turns, takes the firing posture and aims at the dummy, his finger around the trigger. Chikukwa springs to his side and points the muzzle down.

Chikukwa

Gunshots and grieving are incompatible. Even trigger-happy Mapfupa has spared the elephant for a solid week reverence of the mourning.

Dombo

The head of the goat is interred, which means my brother was laid to rest. Clansmen, kith and kin must lead normal lives again. Is there a new ordinance that we should run amok naked until the diviners return?

He quickly aims again and is set to fire but Chikukwa lowers the muzzle again to his dismay.

Chikukwa

My function is to aid and spruce your image in all things. Upon Changamire's misfortune, I preferred retirement, but you recalled me. Now, allow me to perform my obligations without any hindrance.

Dombo rises and hands the gun to him.

Dombo

In recalling you, I see now that I didn't err. *(Pause)* What else were the clansmen concerned with?

Chikukwa

The alleged disappearance of the four wives. Ibwe anticipates the token burial of four heads of goats very soon. Clansmen want to believe they were murdered until proven otherwise. Among us is a cold-hearted killer with the audacity to slay defenceless women. The same assassin killed the embalmer. This coward the Rozvi vow to catch one way or the other. *(Pause)* Without compromise, clansmen

89

seek a full inquiry, and presume you'll recuse yourself, Sir.

Dombo

I'm particular about keeping invidious trash out of my ears. Now, suddenly you're my enemies' mouthpiece. If I were to recuse myself I'd have resigned this kingdom to fulsome anarchy. It is clear anarchists are bent on rendering Urozviland ungovernable. I won't tolerate it!

Chikukwa

As it stands, only an independent inquiry could exonerate you, Sir. The whispers could hinder your ascendancy.

Dombo

(*After a brief thoughtful censure*)

I'm not averse to waiving my royal immunity. But bending to the whims of flagrant commoners would compel me to relinquish state obligations at a crucial time. Whether clansmen regard me as a villain or paragon is of no consequence to me. Make them understand that neither fire nor the vilest storm can stand between me and that throne.

Chikukwa

(*Defiantly*)

Are you going to recuse yourself, Sir?

Dombo

(*Outraged*)

Who sent you, Chikukwa?

Chikukwa

You did; by recalling me, Sir.

Dombo closes the gap between them and peers into Chikukwa's eyes, turns and wanders to the dummy and gazes into its featureless face mindlessly, before turning around once more.

Dombo

Only after I'm satisfied the inquiry won't prejudice my name will I sanction it. (*Gestures towards the table*) I invited you here for a specific reason. (*Crossing to the table*) I presume there are things I must know before assuming power. In your head are secrets no one can understand if not told. Of these tell me.

Chikukwa crosses to the table, too, and sets the gun against it. The two sit facing each other. Dombo sits his back to the dummy. He uncovers the luncheon. Chikukwa rises picks the jar and washes Dombo's hands and his. He sits.

Dombo uncorks the wine bottle with his teeth. They converse over lunch, Dombo using cutlery, Chikukwa his hands.

Chikukwa

Lo Bengula receives a ransom of two hundred cattle annually.
Dombo is stunned; food falls out of his mouth.
The state has shrunk in size and resources. Actually, now, Urovziland is a piteous chiefdom enjoying very little tribute from surrounding chiefs. Certainly you'll seat on the throne as a chief. Perhaps that would mitigate in our favour and see the reduction of the ransom.

Dombo

(Laughs)
We'll acquire guns and horses, and overrun the Amandabili.

Chikukwa

I trust you'll lead your army of tubercular's and drunkards from the front. But be sure to look over your shoulder or only your solitary self will reach Guruuswa.
Chikukwa pops a fruit into his mouth and quickly fills his wine glass, Dombo looks at him hatefully.

Dombo

Mapfupa will come to our assistance. There's a formidable British army across the Limpopo. Mapfupa promised us the service of that army should the Amandabili threaten us. The key to our deliverance lies with the white-skins.

Chikukwa

What a pathetically circuitous way of expressing cowardice!

Dombo

Weigh you words, Chikukwa! I would hate to make a brutal spectacle out of you. This would confuse the prevailing celebratory atmosphere in Ibwe now that a veritable man of commerce is about to take the reigns.

Chikukwa

I'm not a ministering spirit, Sir. The present times are an empty honeycomb. The state needs a leader who'll bring back triumphal celebrations. Skulls ought to be paraded to public applause once again. Chirisamhuru must be vomiting in his tomb.

Dombo

(Sharply)
Don't say that of my father! He was a profound warrior.

91

Regrettably a streak of fate saw him face death at the hands of a woman. Change the subject, I order you, Chikukwa.

Chikukwa

I reiterate that I'm not a ministering spirit. I know the truth. Some elders know this truth, too. But they are few, they are quiet and they are cautious. I prefer that we speak openly and truthfully to each other here before monuments become lies and propaganda as taught by foreigners.

Dombo

What are you talking about?

Chikukwa

Chirisamhuru had two sons, Tohwechipi and Sambabamu. They were the last known heirs. Let us acknowledge the truth first before we build facades to mesmerise the commoner.

Dombo

(Rises)

I will ask you to leave.

Chikukwa

Stop living in the realm of falsehoods and I'll show you your father's grave. *(Solemnly)* Bereft of attention, it's a heap of stones among cacti in a desolate land. He fell in battle. All his wounds were frontal – a gush in the forehead, a pulverised right eye and a slit abdomen. On my shoulders I carried him. But I couldn't carry him far because his stomach and intestines suddenly slipped out. I laid him on the ground. Death began to darken his face. But his tongue was faster than the advent of death. One by one, painstakingly, he mentioned the six of you by name. I still hear his voice in the depths of my ears.

A dumbfounded Dombo stares down at him, arms akimbo.

In that mantra he passed the fire to the six of you, the expression of a dying father's undying affection for his sons. Then he died. *(Rises)* To the man worthy of honour you turn your back. To the shameful legacy of an unworthy king who couldn't defend himself against a woman you cling.

Dombo

(Picks up the gun)

I'll shoot you if you don't leave now.

Chikukwa

A ferocious war raged, but I gave your father's a decent burial. I held his hand as he died. I'm not pleading for my life; doing so isn't my custom.

Dombo

(*Aims at his head*)

If what you speak is the truth, why didn't you bring it to my brother's ears?

Chikukwa

Of Persia, the Roman Empire and Hindus he learnt, but he couldn't pick a cue from his knowledge, otherwise he could have restored this state.

Dombo

What a consoling way to bid farewell to my brother!

Chikukwa

Tell me; how do you mourn a moron?

Incensed, Dombo overturns the table, strewing everything that was upon it. He aims the gun at Chikukwa's head again.

Dombo

If I were you, I'd banish myself from this land and live.

Chikukwa

Kill me and live, Dombo. (*Steps towards him*) I long for an exit out of this asphyxiated ecstasy.

He takes another step and the muzzle touches his brow, stopping him briefly. But he lets out a courageous cry and forcibly steps towards Dombo, forcing the latter to back-off slowly, step by step, knocking his chair as he does so. This way the two slowly move towards the dummy; Dombo's back to it and the muzzle pressed against Chikukwa's brow.

Whenever I faced death like this I killed my adversary.

Dombo

(*Retreating, gun poised*)

Each step you take is a stride on a cheetah's tail.

Chikukwa

(*Still advancing*)

End this shameless existence for me. Shoot and send me to your father. My conscience is clear; I no longer suffer a mortal obligation to him. (*Demands*) Shoot, Dombo! Send me into the spirit world! Your father awaits tales of your pride in his legacy!

93

There're near the dummy when an off-stage commotion catches their attention. Mounting and discordant voices stop them in their movements. Both look off-stage, Dombo lowering the gun. Enter Mmabatho near the dummy, to the two men's shock. Mmabatho is tense and moving backwards cautiously, an assegai poised, a large, decorated ox-shield raised defensively. The hand holding the shield also bears a knobkerrie. Dombo and Chikukwa back off to the back of the hut in the background, i.e. lower-stage right to upper-stage left, where Chikukwa snatches the gun from Dombo and aims it at Mmabatho. Dombo stands behind Chikukwa who assumes a firing posture on one knee.

Mmabatho is a giant in full military regalia of skins and cascading oxtail tassels above his calves and biceps. His soiled feet are in homemade rustic sandals. A leather band around his head supports a towering plume of ostrich feathers. He is still moving cautiously when he turns and sees the two men and the gun poised at him. He halts but faces the direction of his entry. Enter about a dozen warriors with spears and knobkerries poised, in a semi-circle and in vigilant pursuance of Mmabatho. The warriors stop at the edge of the backyard, the dummy and the warrior in their arc. Stranded between two groups, Mmabatho constantly turns to face each in a fervent attempt to defend himself, then he feigns advancing to the warriors. They retreat fearfully, most into off-stage obscurity.

Mmabatho
(*To the warriors*)

You herded me here. Show me the man in charge now that your king is dead!

Dombo
Who're you?

Mmabatho
(*Turns and faces him*)

I'm a Zulu emissary; by rank commander; by name Nduna Ntshingwayo of the Ngobamakhosi regiment. I'm on an ambassadorial mission. I expect a momentous reception. Who're you?

Dombo
Dombo, the heir-apparent. Who sent you?

Mmabatho
The Sky, Cetshwayo, the king of the Zulu and all tribes. He extends conditional peace to you.

Dombo

How do I know you're from King Cetshwayo?

Mmabatho

(*Tilts his head slightly to show him the plumes*)

Can't you see the plume of ostrich feathers? The Sky himself placed it on my head when he charged me with this mission. It took me a full moon to reach this place. Make the atmosphere conducive to diplomatic discussions, or we draw blood unnecessarily. If I don't return to Zululand within the expected period *impis* shall descend on every village, which makes my security and health your concern.

A moment of tense silence prevails.

Dombo

If diplomacy is what you, desire lay down your weapons first.

Mmabatho

A Zulu warrior in battle regalia can't lay down weapons. Besides, I don't bring an accosting embassy. Lay down *your* weapons.

Dombo

If you won't disarm then we won't. What is your embassy, Nduna?

Mmabatho

To avoid obliterating you, King Cetshwayo demands half of all the cattle in this state and three hundred young women. That's all.

Cries of shock from everyone, but weapons remain poised.

Gallant men of this land, keep your women and your cattle. The death you seek you shall find on the tips of assegais. The *impis* shall crack open your skulls. Then we shall take all the cattle and all the beautiful women. Make your choice now; I must return to Zululand.

Dombo

(*Demurs*)

This is a grave matter, Nduna. We'll sit down, ambassador. (*To the rest*) I'll ask all of you to excuse us. Leave.

Chikukwa and the warriors look at Dombo in disbelief.

Return to your posts and don't spread alarm; he comes in peace. You're dismissed!

Exit the warriors, reluctantly. Shaking his head, Chikukwa rises, hands the gun to Dombo and exits, his eyes on Mmabatho. Under the watchful eyes of the visitor, Dombo picks a chair, crosses over to the dummy and sets the chair near it. He backs away cautiously to the overturned table and sits in the chair already facing the dummy. Holding the gun by the stock, he raises it at Mmabatho then places it across his lap. Mmabatho crosses to the vacant chair and sits down, likewise placing his weapons on his lap. The two stare at each other across the backyard.

Mmabatho

Talk. I must return as soon as possible.

Dombo

Your embassy I've heard, but elders must deliberate and take a decision. They could decide that we send our own emissary to King Cetshwayo.

Mmabatho

Sentries will kill your ambassador on sight. Cetshwayo has the blood of Tshaka; he doesn't negotiate.

Dombo

Then, I'll ask you to cool your heels over a couple of days. You'll live in comfort, Nduna. Grant yourself occasion to savour our hospitality.

Mmabatho

Then I must have female company for the duration of my stay.

Dombo

(Taken aback)

It isn't our custom to entertain visitors that way. You should have brought a wife with you.

Mmabatho

An *impi* warrior cannot be married. I insist on a different woman each day for the duration of my stay. In the morning I demand milk and roasted fillet steak. In the afternoon I need millet beer and smoked fish. In the evening I need a proper meal with fowl stew. You could delay me for a week at most.

Speechless, Dombo shakes his head.

Oh! You suppose this is a delusion! Take me to the elders. I have no time to waste with a herd boy. (*Rises, bringing up the shield and poising the assegai*)

Dombo

Sit down, Nduna Ntshingwayo. Consider the demands for your stay met.

Mmabatho's face breaks into a wide smile.

Curtain.

Act IV

Scene 1

26th Day. Afternoon. Sir Wilkie Crowler's sitting room.

(In the wooden room is a set of three cushioned wooden sofas around a low table. In a corner a small display unit exhibits many ethnic sculptures, idolatrous in nature. On the walls are game trophies, skins and a sword among other decorations. There's a main door, an inner one and a panel window, all closed.

Sir Wilkie Crowler on a sofa is examining a piece of rock with the aid of a magnifying glass and a handkerchief. On the table are two small mounds of similar stones, a hammer, a double-barrelled gun, an almost full bottle of whisky and an empty tot glass. Under the table is a small empty sack. He is immaculately dressed in a spotlessly clean and well-pressed khaki tunic, a matching pair of hunter's trousers and polished boots. His hair is close-cropped and oiled. His moustache is distinct; extravagant and buffalo-horn shaped. Belts of cartridges wind over his shoulders like sashes and overlap below his chest.

Presently, he spits on the stone, polishes the spot vigorously with the handkerchief and scrutinises it through the magnifying glass. Sudden prolonged knocking on the main door jerks him away from his task. Promptly, he shoves the magnifying glass into his breast pocket, quickly scoops all the rocks and the hammer in the sack, and shoves it in the small gap between the sofa and the wall. He carries out a quick inspection and wipes the table with the handkerchief. The next instant he is lounging leisurely in the sofa, legs propped on the table, the gun across his lap.)

Crowler

Come in!

Enter Rev. Holbrook in horse-riding attire, a straw sun hat in his hand. As he opens the door incoherent traditional singing accompanied by a dreary drumbeat fills the room. Closure of the door behind him kills the noise. Crowler puts the gun on the table and rises.

Rev. Holbrook! What a pleasant surprise! Welcome, Sir.

Holbrook

(Crossing to him and shaking his hand firmly)

It's good to see you again, Sir Wilkie Crowler. I was on pastoral visits and thought I stop by and see how you're coping.

Crowler

That's considerate of you, Reverend. Please sit down and feel at home. I'll be with you presently.

Holbrook sits on a sofa and places his hat on the armrest of the third one. Crowler exits through the inner door, from which he emerges with an unopened wine bottle and a glass and plays butler to the reverend. Holbrook raises his hands in modest protest.

(*Smiling*) No need to panic, Reverend. The wine is Eucharistic. Probably the very quality our Lord produced at Cana.

He sets the glass and the bottle before the reverend and resumes his seat. Holbrook picks up the bottle, reads the label and nods consent. From a pocket Crowler takes out a cork-screw and opens the bottle. He fills Holbrook's glass, lightly corks the bottle and sets it on the table. He fixes himself a tot of whisky, gulps it and grimaces. Holbrook takes a hesitant sip and sets his glass down.

Holbrook

Tastes somewhat like chocolate and syrup... good, actually.

Crowler

I always keep a treatise for everyone. Is there anything you'd particularly want me to do for you, Reverend?

Holbrook

Not at all, Sir Crowler. Just thought I should stop in for a chat. Thought, too, you might be missing the horse, otherwise this is purely a courtesy call which I will cut short should you be occupied.

Crowler

The horse is a thoroughbred accustomed to tough conditions and neglect. Just make sure you take him on a long canter and a full gallop whenever possible. Chances are you'll keep him. Wait a week, then you can celebrate your acquisition.

Holbrook

That'll be generous of you, Sir Crowler.

Crowler

How's the church doing?

Holbrook

It's flourishing, I must say. Membership swells daily. Already a rustic prayer house stands at the site. Numerous huts have been erected. Bands of men are clearing a large tract of land for farming. I can't wait to inform my Archbishop in England.

Crowler

Oh! Archbishop Stanford Lichfield. I know him personally.

Holbrook

Oh, you do!

Crowler

I know a lot of important personalities in England, including some knights, which prompts me to aspire for knighthood. Tell me more about your progress, Reverend.

Holbrook

The station has become a haven for dwarfs, twins, albinos and the severely crippled. About thirty of them are residing at the station – all between a month and fifteen years.

Crowler

One wonders where they were being kept; the custom is to kill them at birth. (*Squinting his eyes*) This might translate to thirty convictions of condemnation. Little wonder there's now palpable tension between believers and non-believers. Seemingly, two antagonistic states have emerged. There's a lot of talk, a lot of bitterness.

Holbrook

What are the people saying?

Crowler

Very unpleasant things, Reverend. If the hardcore traditionalists were better organised, a rampaging brigade of militias would've paid you a visit before now. They plan to hold machetes to your members' throats and ask them to denounce Christ. How big is your membership?

Holbrook

About a third of the populace.

Crowler

A third of the populace can constitute an army. There're dangerous developments taking place. The rapid growth of your church is one of them. A Zulu warrior is in our midst. I would advice you to be armed always. Encourage all the converts to be armed as well.

Holbrook

I appreciate your concern, Sir Crowler. But our God is called the Lord of Sabaoth. (*Sighs and shrugs*) I came across the Zulu warrior yesterday. He was dead drunk and dragging a helpless woman. What's he after?

Crowler

He came to collect half the kingdom's cattle and three hundred young women. Dombo approached me for counsel. I told him to delay the brute for as long as possible.

Holbrook

(*Bewildered*)

How did you become popular with the royal family?

Crowler

(*Smiles*)

Oh, simple, by gathering bones.

Holbrook

What bones, Sir Crowler?

Crowler

This is a land of superstitions. Remember the medium and his assistant who died about three and a half weeks ago.

Holbrook

(*Nods*)

Ronda-*something* and his acolyte?

Crowler

I hadn't yet arrived, but I was told that vultures chased away elders from the shrine and feasted on the bodies. The vultures were huge and many. They ate all the flesh. People watched from a distance as hyenas and jackals joined the party, a terrible feast marked by shrieks, growls and barking according to eye-witnesses. When it was over, the two men's bones were strewn on the entire acreage of the shrine. I was told the bones lay forlorn for a number of days.

Holbrook

I was told that for the natives to have left the shrine in such a state was grossly negligent. But it was taboo for them to touch the bones.

Crowler

Then along comes Crowler. These natives wanted a non-Rozvi to perform the task of janitor. I offered to help, went there and handpicked every bone. I tried to construct the individual skeletons but the bones were of the same size. I buried the bones in one grave in the shrine. That's all. It pleased them and I earned a nickname —Mapfupa. It means *bones*.

Holbrook

You were in the limelight of Providence.

Crowler

(*Fills the tot glass again and rises with it*)

The air is getting stuffy.

He crosses to the panel window while Rev. Holbrook sips his wine. At the wall he turns and faces his visitor.

When do we see a modern missionary station at the site?

Holbrook

Parsonical gothic shall replace the anomalous constructions once I travel to England. The church building shall be striking and ornamental with a high-columned portico and a sky-reaching pinnacle. England will avail everything, and is ready to do so.

Crowler

A splendid mini-Vatican City it shall be, I'm sure, but ill-assorted in a sea of disreputable dwellings.

Holbrook

The Lord's Ark is ever eye-catching. With time we shall raise the standards of the community to match the station. Schools and universities will take care of that.

Crowler

You seem to see far into the future, Reverend. (*Drains the tot in one gulp and grimaces again*) This ill-favoured place lacks everything Britain has. (*Faces the wall. Unlatches the panel*) I hate this place. It dissipates a man's spirit.

He swings open the window, and music offstage fills the room. Sorrowful, and incoherent it is accompanied by drumbeat, wailing and a tinkling hand bell. The noise fades, depicting the group's passage. Sir Crowler looks out the window.

The bumpkins are bringing back the spirit of a dead relation. What did God have in mind when he created these blockheads? I can single out some members of your congregation, Reverend. I know some of them. The cautious have smeared themselves with ashes and red ochre. Gaiety and physical structure betray the disguised ones. Everyone is assuredly resigned to the spirits. These are long time favourites of the Devil.

Holbrook

Most are still grappling with their old selves.

Crowler
(*Still looking out the window*)
This Christ whom you preach, Rev. Holbrook, can he replace the love of the dead in an African heart? Can these orgiasts and barbarians and pagans truly worship God?

Holbrook
No one is completely irreclaimable.
Sir Crowler turns and crosses to the display unit.

Crowler
(*As if speaking to the sculptures*)
Idolaters, that's what these people are… indefatigably married to the spirit-elders. (*Lifts a fierce-looking sculpture from the unit, one with beads and oversized features, and appraises it*) My long stint in West Africa with the Igbo, the Yoruba and the Fulani tells me that these savages shall one day turn against you. Once they receive enough influence from the other world your church members shall decapitate you.
He takes the sculpture to the table and sets it before the Reverend. The noise from outside dies down completely.
(*Looking down at the curving*) One of my priceless souvenirs from West Africa! I salvaged it from a missionary's bonfire after its surrender from a herbalist. He had practised as a Christian for three years. This piece brought fertility.

Holbrook
I think I must take my leave, Sir Crowler. (*Drains his glass and puts it down*) Thanks for a remarkable afternoon.

Crowler
Take no offence, Rev. Holbrook. I only sought to make you more wary. An abrupt departure would be rude and unwarranted. The Queen of Great Britain is of the order of Melchizedek, which makes these natives enemies of God and Britain.
He refills his tot glass with whisky, Holbrook's with wine. He resumes his seat.
I must discuss with you a matter of great urgency and importance.

Holbrook
I'm listening.

Crowler
Before I left England, the Crown, through the Foreign Office for African Affairs, instructed me to trace and locate you. Queen

Victoria has a particularly high regard for missionaries. The Archbishop of England reports to her directly; hence, she knew about your voyage to these parts.

Holbrook

It never occurred to me that my work here would concern the Crown.

Crowler

Matters political and matters spiritual concern the Queen. It's her duty to protect and shepherd the shepherds.

Holbrook

That's spiritually uplifting. I feel closer to God than before.

Crowler

Closer to God and the British Crown, if I may correct you, Reverend. (*Quickly gulps the tot, grimaces and puts the glass on the table beside the sculpture*) These natives should thank God I was able to locate you.

Holbrook
(*Astonished*)

Why?

Crowler

Had they harmed or killed you my order was to instruct British regiments across the Limpopo to exterminate these pagans. It's undocumented British policy to safeguard and avenge the lives of all British missionaries.

Holbrook

I'm not sure whether or not this should impress me. May God give us the grace not to be more barbaric than the barbarians. What exactly is your occupation, Sir Crowler?

Crowler

I'm an asset of the Crown furthering British interests abroad. I didn't study War & Politics at the University of London to come here and shoot elephants. You can call me a spy, a pathfinder or a passive ambassador.

Holbrook

I suspected as much.

Crowler
(*Rising*)

Excuse me, Reverend.

Exit Sir Crowler through the inner door, only to re-merge with a neatly folded Union Jack, like a baby. A pace into the room he stands at attention. (Motionless) The Queen wants this land, all of it. The Queen relies on her subjects, you and me, to achieve her objective. This Union Jack must flap in the winds here, or we would have failed her majesty dismally.

Rev. Holbrook staring at him, he ceremoniously unfolds the flag and drapes it over his left shoulder, then stands at ease.

Holbrook

I refuse to be drawn into your political machinations. I'm sorry.

Crowler

I stood by you when you were in dire need. Is this how you thank me, Reverend?

Holbrook

Was it conditional? What do you want me to do?

Crowler

Rev. Abraham Holbrook, I beseech you. Don't go for the herrings. Go for the whale, that one-off haul that will put you permanently out of the water. Preach Christ to this one man – Dombo. Then preach Dombo to your converts. Popular, he'll be appointed king. Docile, he'll give our army a hassle-free entry into this land. We already enjoy his trust and will take this land without shedding a single drop of blood. Help me campaign for him.

Holbrook

I have neither the genius nor head for politics. Besides, it would be heresy for me to preach a mortal man. I don't want to be the one to bring Armageddon.

Crowler suddenly seems to remember something. He goes to the sofa on which he sat, spreads the flag on its backrest and from under the table pulls out the sack which he places at Rev. Holbrook's feet. The Reverend looks inside the sack takes out some rocks, which he examines. Crowler squats beside him.

Crowler

Gold, Reverend. High quality gold! It's everywhere in abundance. The natives have little use for it and trample it blindly. We'll mine it by the bucket and ship it by the ton. This is the break anyone craves in life. The missionary station will never lack anything. You and I will name this country together.

Holbrook

Yes, the gold is visible. (*Drops the rocks*) But I refuse to lend myself to your ambitions. I'm sorry, Sir Crowler. (*Rises*) Good day, Sir.
Crowler reaches for the gun and straightens up. The men stare at each other, the air suddenly tense. Crowler places a hand on Rev. Holbrook's shoulder and forces him down into the sofa.
What're you doing? Are you going to kill me?

Crowler
(*Growling, looking down at him*)
You're a man of God. I'm a man of war. Both of us are children of God. This is 1875. Queen Victoria is on the throne….

Holbrook

Sir Crowler, if you have nothing new to say do not waste my time. I know this is 1875. This is the Victorian Age.
Crowler sighs throws the gun onto the third sofa and sits on the one on whivh the Union Jack is draped.

Crowler

Sorry I manhandled you, Rev. Holbrook. Don't get the impression I'm using bull-dog tactics on you. Give these natives an opportunity to enjoy gramophones, telephones, motor cars…. (*Pause*) Don't be so hard-hearted. Pity these ape-men. They're in dire need of civilisation. A harbinger of war is in the village. Across the veldt the Ndebele are precariously quiet. Our political and religious efforts will go up in smoke.

Holbrook

Sir Crowler, you work to weird motivations. I've already declined as modestly as possible. Can I go now?

Crowler

You could be at logger heads with colonialism, but by your actions you effectively sign these natives' death warrant. Plan A, with its amicability, has been foiled by the Reverend – congratulations! Now I must resort to Plan B.

Holbrook

What's Plan B, if I may know?

Crowler

A full-scale attack by four British regiments. We'll poison the rivers with cyanide, lay a preliminary siege then attack from the four cardinal points. I shall personally coordinate the attack as in Bombay and other numerous West African campaigns. We'll wipe the Rozvi from the face of the earth!

Holbrook

Christ! You delight in killing… in stealing from God! You're an atrocity, Crowler!

Crowler

It's you who delights in blood. You preach with passion only to turn out a mortifying hypocrite at the end! After the bombardment I'll send a report to your Archbishop. I'm confident my good friend, Sir Stanford Lichfield, will not be too pleased with you. Pray you perish in the attack! (*Pause. Voice now tremulous with rage*) Man of God, my house and the villages are now out of bounds to you! Leave my horse behind; I wouldn't want to drop you from that saddle with a bullet through the head.

Sir Crowler rises grabs the gun and crosses over to the panel window.
(*Shouts out the window*) Manjombo!…Manjombozi! (*Brief pause*) Unsaddle Commonwealth! He's going nowhere! Throw the damn saddle in!

He leaves the window and comes to stand beside the flag-draped sofa.
Good day, Holbrook. We shall not meet again except in Hell.

Rev. Holbrook demurs dumbfounded. He reaches for his hat and rises. The Reverend stretches out a hand, but Sir Crowler ignores it. Rev. Holbrook bows slightly and walks slowly towards the main door. As he approches the door a saddle with stirrups sails into the room through the window and lands behind him with a thud. Startled, he stops and turns.

Crowler

If it is martyrdom you seek let Dombo change his attitude towards me. I'll ride to that forest and turn you inside-out. I swear to God I mean it!

Holbrook

Let's keep the Holy One out of this painful conversation. Precious in the sight of the Lord is the death of his saints.

Crowler

I'll make sure those words are captured on your gravestone.

Exit Rev. Holbrook. Sir Crowler remains staring at the door.

Curtain.

Scene 2

28th Day. Late evening. Chapwanya's sitting-hut.

(A one circular wall affair of poles and clay. Two kerosene lamps light the room. Sitting on stools are Chapwanya, Chinake and Gungwa, head bowed and elbows on his knees. Chinake is holding a snuff container.)

Chinake
Chikukwa converted this afternoon, and was immediately baptised in that ditch of water near his homestead. When he was set to be immersed an ancestral spirit took possession of him. The spirit protested violently, threatening to kill Chikukwa forthwith. But Holbrook immersed him all the same to the amusement of onlookers. The spirit cried miserably and left him.

Chapwanya
Did Chikukwa surrender the curios of his personal shrine?

Chinake
He surrendered nothing. *(Pause)* General Gwenhere is dead.

Chapwanya
(Calmly)
Yes, he's finally dead. I've always maintained that cowardice and mutiny are only punishable by death.

Chinake
He tried to fast for forty days and forty nights, and died on the fourth day – today. This new religion is dangerous.

Chapwanya
Death is thorough. Everything is at its disposal. This new faith would be good if only it could be reconciled with our traditional beliefs. The precepts *thou shall not kill, thou shall not steal* are ancestral. But love, kindness and meekness turn a vicious warrior into a feeble woman.

Chinake
There's a Zulu in Ibwe. We should be preparing for war, yet clansmen heedlessly convert and die. The *nduna* cannot have trekked alone. Perhaps *impis* have already taken strategic positions around the city. There are no diviners to counter the fetishes that make the *impis* invisible.

Chapwanya
(*Lugubriously*)
Clansmen are overawed; me, too. They can't hide their fear when they look at the *nduna*. I'm not afraid of the *nduna*, but of the fact that we won't take up arms.

Chinake
Clansmen are considering exile.

Chapwanya
I want to bludgeon the Zulu, but I lack the nerve and wonder if it's the right thing to do. Exile would be injurious to my self-esteem. For our cause I must stay. Maybe this is the time to bury our differences with Dombo and mount a monstrous resistance.

Chinake
We could ask Dombo to make the *nduna* an irresistible offer; Bribe him with a reasonable herd and a pretty wife or two. Then ask him to inform Cetshwayo that our cattle are scraggy and our women skeletal and disease-ridden.

Chapwanya
Cetshwayo isn't foolish. He'll gather his soothsayers to hear the *nduna's* report. The *nduna* will be killed that very day. The Zulu are more savage than the Amandabili. Gungwa must go into exile as soon as possible.

Chinake
That's my opinion, too. Danger comes from the south; the leeway is in the north. Beyond the Zambezi is the Bemba, a hospitable people.

Chapwanya
Therefore I'll take him and some homage gifts to the king of the Bemba. Once he's accepted I'll return whether Urozviland is in turmoil or not. We ought to contribute towards Gungwa's welfare abroad. Cattle would make our departure conspicuous. Let's convert our livestock into gold nuggets. Within the week we must leave.

Chinake
(*To Gungwa*)
Abroad suffer no nostalgia. Nothing here is worth missing. Don't languish, but sojourn as a king apprentice. Return a restorer.

His head bowed, Gungwa hardly stirs. A brief silence, then Rev. Holbrook's voice off-stage makes them sit up, Gungwa, too. They exchange bewildered glances throughout the Reverend's off-stage eclectic presentation.

Holbrook's Voice

(*An off-stage eclogue rising to a crescendo*)
Woe to the rebellious children, saith the Lord
That take counsel, but not of me.
Isaiah said it; the fiery serpent shall come from the south.
And warned them; ferry your riches, but to a people of no profit.
Sit still, said the voice, your strength is in knowing I'm God.

Gungwa rises and listens intently, head inclined to the right where the voice is coming from. The eclogue continues.

Though the Lord gives you the bread of adversity
He'll be gracious at the voice of your cry.
In that day the light of seven days shall be upon the land.
Your fat and plenteous cattle shall feed in large pastures.

Chapwanya

What a riotous challenge! The spirit-elders roam in the coolness of the night. Now with Holbrook taking every opportunity to spread alarm their nocturnal peace is violated. Who'll stop this demon?

Chinake

Just what is this Christianity, Chapwanya? Is it a mere brutalised man hanging on a tree?

Chapwanya

Cursed is everyone who hangs himself or is hanged. And the Rozvi pretend not to know it. Custom forbids us to touch the corpses of hanged men, worse still worship such! The converts invite calamity on behalf of the innocent.

Brief clapping is heard off-stage. Gungwa resumes his seat, and his former subdued posture. Enter Gundu.

Gundu

(*Stepping inside*)
You won't believe this. No one envisaged it. I don't know whether we should celebrate or mourn. (*Stops and looks down at the elders*) Mapfupa and the baVenda brutes have vanished!

Chapwanya

They could've gone hunting. You can't be sure, Gundu. Sit down.

Gundu

They've vanished with everything they brought! The only thing left is the wooden house. But that awe-inspiring house is burning as we speak.

The elders and Gungwa express shock. The adolescent bows his head again.
The sheer size of the inferno is attracting onlookers. We rushed to investigate, and found the house maliciously battered and ferociously aflame. The house is a burning empty shell. The horses, the ivory, the furniture, everything is gone.

Chapwanya

By daybreak when Mapfupa can be trailed he would've ridden beyond five horizons. Whenever they rest they shall lie in ambush. Trailing him would be tantamount to pursuing a viper into its borough.

Chinake

But can we continue to leave Dombo to his devises? Let's prevail upon him to mobilize the army. The armies of the vassal chiefdoms could afford us a concerted resistance. We'll give the *impis* a relentless pursuit to Zululand. We must take the war to Cetshwayo, and kill that devil too.

Gundu

Over the years we lost all vassalages to the Amandabili except that of the Ndau. But what the Ndau deem an army is a mob of emancipated *muchongoyo* dancers. It's sensible we leave them alone, otherwise they might delude us into thinking our army is big.

Chinake

Most of our warriors have converted. Because they won't fight alongside pagans, they won't help us defend our land.

Gundu

But does Holbrook's Christ make them immune to a Zulu attack?

Chapwanya

No one enjoys immunity; even the distributor of amulets is shaking. A solitary warrior ravages our women, trampling our dignity. I can't bear the humiliation anymore.

Chinake

So far seven women have been abused. Dombo has been seizing them from their families with the assistance of the baVenda brutes. One of the victims was a drooling autistic. But it appears the *nduna* was too drunk to notice it. Such excesses in permissiveness spell a forfeiture of rainfall for many years. I have never seen such manifestation of bestial libido in a man! And the animal indulges in his impromptu embassy at Dombo's homestead.

111

Gundu
When drunk the menace turns into an oracular whirlwind. Everyday he ambulates restlessly. He has been to every village of the citadel. Whenever he opens his mouth he broadcasts words that induce diarrhoea. Everyone, including children, now knows that there's a Zulu *nduna* in Ibwe; namely Ntshingwayo; regiment Ngombamakhosi; the issue, cattle and three hundred women.

Chinake
He says they'll wash our blood off their assegais in their sacred Thukela River. He swears they'll behead Dombo and take his head across the Limpopo for the Zulu gods to savour their victory.

Chapwanya
But one warrior doesn't constitute an *impi*. Tomorrow we kill the amorous ambassador. I'll chop him down myself with my battle-axe. One stroke to the temple and everyone will wake up to the call for war.

Off-stage brief clapping. Enter Makeredza confounded.

Chinake
Sit down, Makeredza. We heard it all; Mapfupa has fled with everything. His house is burning.

Makeredza
Then you haven't heard it all…an act most hideous, a sight most haunting. (*Sighs and shakes his head*) Dombo is dead.
Gungwa lifts his head, shocked. The elders look up at Makeredza mouths agape. (*Emphatically*) Dombo is dead.

Gundu
What happened?

Makeredza
I'm coming from his homestead. His body dangles from the roof of his sleeping-hut. It's a grisly spectacle. He's disembowelled, his right eye gorged out, and there's a ghastly wound on his forehead. When I saw his corpse I thought I was dreaming.

Chinake
(*Contentedly*)
What is the extent of the spirits' anger?

Gungwa
Are you really sure, vaMakeredza?

Makeredza

I'm sorry to break such news to you, son. He hangs from the apex... killed quickly and quietly. His wives heard nothing though they were in their huts. The horror gags them from wailing. Abdominal organs hang outside the body.

Gungwa

I don't know how to react to this, frankly. I'll let it sink in first. (*Bows his head again*)

Chapwanya

Were there faecal deposits below the corpse?

Makeredza

Nothing save a few drops of blood. The wounds were almost bloodless. His wives said the pile of ivory he kept in the same hut was missing.

He was murdered. But which fool would overkill him?

Chapwanya

This night is decisive. It dangerously re-sculptures everything. (*A short contemplative pause*) Kuvaronza-the-Beast takes over as the heir-apparent. (*Reminiscing*) Former hard-drinker... public brawler... seducer of minors... wife-butcher – deservedly earned himself the sobriquet *Beast*. His name fills my mouth with bile.

Gundu

He's worse than Dombo though he converted on the dusk of the sermon on the scaffold.

Makeredza

The beast fell on his knees and vowed to avenge his brother. He is adamant only non-believers are capable of committing such a heinous murder. Initially his prime suspect was Mapfupa, but upon learning of his disappearance he shifted the blame to all the heathens. Swearing by the relics of his ancestors, he said every heathen shall fall by his machete and those of other believers. Clansmen who had gathered in the homestead quickly left. (*Sits*)

Chinake

The holy fool has chosen to spark the inferno that will consume the Christians. Let him blunder. Keep your weapons within reach.

Chapwanya

Every arrival is bringing us bad news tonight. I wonder if some occurrence is holding Nyamaropa, or he himself is dead.

113

Off-stage shrieking punctuated with the tinkling of a hand-bell captures their attention. The noise dies suddenly and is replaced by a metallic booming male voice in an apparent oracular public address.

Oracular Voice

O, augur, emerge; the cry of the vulture is itinerant.

A dark dawn comes, of calamity and no remnant

The anthem of conquest has become a forgotten relic

The battle-cry crier you rendered forlorn and antique

Panic; the flamer-thrower stands near your hut.

No sacrifice will suffice, no supplication will atone the heart

This is my appeal to bowed and sudden amputees

Once a roaring pride, now spectators of Palm trees.

Voice falls silent

Chinake

This night is like no other night. First it was Holbrook, now this.

Makeredza

I can't place this voice. This could be a returnee diviner. Then every mystery will be demystified in a few days.

Gundu

This voice is enigmatic. It sounds like the ghost of Rondangozi. It also dangerously sounds like Chemusango speaking. Who speaks to Ibwe?

Chapwanya

(Lamentably)

Mapfupa shouldn't have buried Rondangozi and his acolyte in the same grave. It's taboo. And Mwari's shrine isn't a graveyard. The white-skin erred most gravely. Now, we must suffer spectral visitations.

Oracular Voice

Where's the avowed unstoppable warrior?

Where're the clansmen of old, who swore to perish in battle?

Fear deadens the voice of the battle-cry crier.

Now that you marvel and unashamedly cower

Drink to your adversary's victory

Accept without flinching his banditry

Stand guard while he molests your daughters.

Find him the harshest aphrodisiac to prolong his laughter.

Voice falls silent again.

Gundu

The voice is vaguely familiar. But the accent is almost alien. This could be an ideal replacement spirit. Perhaps, one too archaic to utter with ease modern words? Now we'll be taken out of this quagmire.

Oracular Voice

(Diminishing)

But since you've chosen to be ensnared by your imagination
Northward is the flamingo's flight from drought and ruination.
The hawk ceaselessly shrieks your dirge
Gyrate not, but turn your back on your prestige
Pack the black cloth, and wave at the ancestral graves.
North, plead with the amiable Bemba and the Lozi
Lo! Further north halt, ho! Hutu and Tutsi danger!
Barbed arrows poised, they perilously linger.

Again off-stage hand-bell tolling follows, diminishing, too.

Chinake

This is a clear call to exile.

Chapwanya

If it's Rondangozi calling, we can't heed a ghost. If it's a returnee medium then it's a coward's call. If it's Chemusango, then death calls. *Silence. Hasty clapping off-stage. Enter Nyamaropa, wide-eyed. The elders look up at him expectantly.*

Nyamaropa

You heard the oracle?

Chapwanya

Yes, Nyamaropa, and Holbrook, too... loud and clear.

Nyamaropa

Dombo is dead. Mapfupa has fled. The wooden house is burning. What's our resolution?

Chinake

We're glad you bear no more disturbing news. What took you so long?

Nyamaropa

I was on my way here when I came across a party of thirteen disgruntled men, all close kin of the *nduna's* victims, all swearing death to the Zulu, all armed with spears and machetes. I joined them. We went to Dombo's homestead only to find the host

115

hanging from his roof and the savage absent. A manhunt began. From thirteen our number swelled to about forty as we roamed.

Chapwanya

Is the Zulu dead? Or all of you shook upon seeing him.

Nyamaropa

We couldn't find him. The Zulu has disappeared, too. We went everywhere, but then the oracular voice sent clansmen scurrying homewards. New spirits are often short-tempered and curse at the slightest opportunity. (*Sits on a stool and sighs*) Instinct tells me the brute is gone. Juju forewarned him.

Makeredza

You heard the spirit's call. What do you say, Nyamaropa?

Nyamaropa

My family and I are leaving this land tomorrow. My heart urges me to leave. I've always listened to my heart.

The elders stare at him as if spooked. Gungwa remains noncommittal.

I'm sorry, elders, but I cannot? remain supportive of our cause. Half of my cattle I'll take with me. Along the way I might convert some of them into gold or portable items. The remainder of the beasts I'll gamble with at the Zambezi River. The hippopotami and the crocodiles will grab some, but some will make it, spirits willing. Beyond the Zambezi, I leave it to the ancestors.

Gundu

What becomes of half of the wealth you'll leave?

Nyamaropa

I donate it to the cause, whole-heartedly, the homestead and everything. About sixty cattle are all yours if you're staying. Perhaps those who stay will survive. Perhaps those in exile will make it. Perhaps I'll perish abroad. I heard the few who are choosing to stay say they'll convert at daybreak. (*Pauses and sighs*) If I elect to stay the temptation to convert might overwhelm me. Of the two evils — conversion and exile, the latter appeals to me.

Chapwanya

(*Gravely saddened*)

What has disarmed the scorpion?

Nyamaropa

The Rozvi army is now a pathetic, jaundiced torso. The remaining commanders will freak and defecate on hearing the Zulu war-cry.

116

Chinake

But for this reason we came together, Nyamaropa.

Nyamaropa

If it takes thirteen men to confront one Zulu warrior wearied by fornication, what should be the ideal size of the Rozvi army that can repel an *impi* vanguard? Stay and defend the land, but this land is no longer worth dying for. (*Rises*) For tomorrow's exodus I must prepare. Farewell, elders. Again, I say farewell.

Exit Nyamaropa leaving everyone head bowed. A long silence ensues.

Gungwa

(*Suddenly looks up and rises*)

I've been pondering since yesterday. I saw my father when he was beginning to ail. Haemorrhaging from all orifices and scars preceded the stiffness. Logic no longer has a place here.

Chapwanya

What're you driving at, son?

Gungwa

I've neither portion nor honour in this land. I'm not a thief and I'm not going into exile.

The elders growl, astounded.

If anything, my heartfelt sympathy goes to the rightful dynastic family wallowing in obscurity. Tomorrow I'm converting. Perhaps there's solace in Holbrook's Christ. My mind is made up. I'm sorry, elders.

Chapwanya

(*Shaking with rage and rising*)

Get out of my sight, you miserly coward!

Chapwanya is about to slap Gungwa, who recoils, brings his hands up. Chapwanya points at the door as the elders rise to restrain him. Exit Gungwa shaking his head. The elders stare at the door after him.

Curtain.

Scene 3

31ˢᵗ Day. Daybreak. The missionary station, Chikasha Forest.

(From behind the closed curtain comes the noise of a raid underway; battle cries and wails of the attacked, mostly women. Fervent whistling, the noise of crumbling structures and ceaseless mooing and bleating accompany the tumult. Suddenly all other noises except the cries of livestock die down. A whistle, and the noise of a raging attack starts all over. But the number of the screams of the attacked is fast fading. The screams die completely moments later. The dwindling cries of livestock being herded away follow until all is quiet.

The curtain opens to reveal an overrun scene; smouldering and crumbled primitive buildings, scattered household effects and many corpses, all bloodied and lying in various awkward positions. In the foreground among the dead are: the eight porters, Chikukwa, Shannon and Gungwa.

Rev. Holbrook lies prostrate and motionless in the background, an assegai protruding from the top of his left shoulder close to the neck. He begins to groan and grunt, and rises painstakingly. His cream shirt is torn and bloodied in several places. Wobbling and vainly trying to reach the assegai whose blade is embedded in his back, he falls to the ground only to rise again in the same manner as before. Staggering and in traumatic shock, one hand groping, the other vainly attempting to reach the assegai, he manoeuvres slowly in the rubble and corpses until he comes to the foreground. He discovers the body of Shannon and sinks to his knees beside it. With mounting difficulty he checks the body for signs of life – pries the eyes open and gazes into them, feels for a pulse in the neck and both wrists, and desperately massages her cheeks in a bid to revive her. He struggles to his feet again, only to fall and fail to rise.

Enter Chemusango in the background, in his usual black, the calabashes strapped by his sides. Appraising the damage and the dead indifferently, he wanders in the rubble until he comes to Rev. Holbrook, and looks down at him with the same indifference. A moment later he turns away, returns to his point of entry and picks up a machete. Fingering its cutting edge, he returns to the Reverend. Squatting, he grabs a handful of Rev. Holbrook's hair, pulls his head from the ground and is set to cut off his head when a noise from behind makes him stop and turn.

Enter Mmabatho with about a dozen impi warriors who quickly surround the hermit, assegais poised. The hermit rises, the machete in hand. Rev. Holbrook is motionless.)

Mmabatho

The last Rozvi standing! A death-defying fetish man, I presume. What confronts us?

Chemusango

(*Pointing at him with the machete*)

You maim and kill in my land without hindrance. Who are you?

Mmabatho

Urozviland is ablaze. The Rozvi lie dead in defeat. The whole night we routed the villages. Yet you profess ignorance of who we are. Stubborn goat, disclose your identity or the assegais will silence you forever!

Chemusango

Not until you tell me who you are.

Mmabatho

(*Appraises him rudely, almost going round him*)

The dress and the defiance speak something to me. I presume you're the hermit. If you are, it might please you to hear that your escapades have reached the ears of *Ihlabantu* –Lo Bengula – in Cubulawayo. If you are he, then you're an asset to the Black Calf. Are you the hermit?

Chemusango

You stand close to your death! Answer me first.

Mmabatho

Oh, you threaten an *nduna* and his *impi*!

Mmabatho shakes his head pitiably, turns and wanders in the rubble until he gets to an overturned chair, which he sets right and sits on facing away from the surrounded hermit. The warriors maintain their positions and attacking stances.

Chemusango

You're here to fulfil my prophetic dream. I dreamt of hawks scooping me to their nest. Let's get this over with; a long journey awaits.

Mmabatho

(*Boastfully into the other direction*)

I'm Nduna Mmabatho, alias Ntshingwayo, of the Ndebele Imbezu regiment, one of many wasting your kingdom. Alone I came; the lone leopard that masqueraded as an emissary from Cetshwayo, King of the Zulu.

Mmabatho

I saw you in my abode. You held out libido to distract scrutiny. Tactics and espionage is your domain. (*Pause*) In the secret recesses of the mountain I heard your voice broadcasting the flamingo's flight northwards.

Mmabatho
(*Laughs*)

Clansmen were fooled. They left their heritage undefended. This state shall never rise again. I have express instructions from the Black Calf regarding a recluse. Ndebele sorcerers gave me a profile, which I must match with your personal account. Asset or garbage, prove yourself.

Chemusango

I'm a roving spirit. I minister to myself. I'm a foggy teardrop in a gourd full of water.

Mmabatho

Speak plainly, prisoner! Figurative arrogance versus assegais, what would prevail?

Chemusango

Impi or wizard, no man can hold me hostage. Order your warriors to lay down their weapons.

Mmabatho
(*Without looking back*)

Crouch, *impi*!
The warriors crouch at once, leaving Chemusango towering.

Mmabatho

You've found Ndangana, the illegitimate son of Chirisamhuru. Nyamazana, the dishonourable female warrior slew my father forty-five years ago. My mother was the right-hand maid of Chirisamhuru's wife. But my mother became pregnant by the king. The royal wives suspecting fowl-play demanded to know the man responsible from my mother. She feared for her life and banished herself from the land. My maternal kinsmen gave her refuge in distant Ndauland.

Mmabatho

I hear you well. Go on.

Mmabatho

I was born and raised in exile. My mother died when I was a toddler. A few years later Nyamazana killed my father. Her warriors massacred the royal family. My half-brothers, Tohwechipi and Sambabamu, survived the attack because it took place in their absence.

Mmabatho

Tell me about the mystic powers.

Chemusango

I grew up without honour. In my boyhood I lamented my father whom I'd never seen. Eventually he came to me in dreams. Faceless figures escorted him. They taught me mantras night after night, which drove me into the forest when I reached adolescence. The bulb of the wild orchid was made edible to me. I was taught to enchant the mamba and converse with the ugly salamander. They led me to sacred, secretive combs. In hallowed catacombs lay pools seething with anthrax and render-pest and Ebola. And they showed me the legume, the antidote to the lethal germs. In my calabashes I sometimes carry milk and honey, but often death.

Mmabatho

(Thoughtfully, still looking away)

Supernatural powers and divination, Lo Bengula will cherish. (*Turns and looks at him*) But your heir ship sounds like a death sentence. In Cubulawayo the Great Black Calf will decide your fate in the blink of an eye. (*To the impi*) Abduct him! Grab the wizard!

The impi *springs and closes in on him. Chemusango drops the machete.*

Chemusango

Don't expend your strength restraining me. I'm an honourable man; I'll walk with dignity.

Mmabatho

Walk then, evil one!

Mmabatho watches rooted to the spot as Chemusango leads the impi away. Exit Chemusango and the impi. Mmabatho nods his content and follows. Exit Mmabatho. In the foreground Rev. Holbrook raises his head cautiously. He crawls away a little, struggles to his knees and assumes a posture of prayer.

Final curtain.

Glossary of Rozvi & Zulu Words

Changamire ------------- Reverent title for Rozvi kings.

Chikara ------------------ A Rozvi awe-inspiring god, bringer of good and bad.

Ihlabantu ---------------- Men-eater; one of Lo Bengula's nicknames (Zulu/Ndebele).

Impi ---------------------- Special Zulu / Ndebele army unit of commandos / corps. (Zulu)

Mfecane ------------------ 'Time of suffering' marked by the flight of Sotho and Nguni-speaking tribes northwards and across the Limpopo River from the wrath and raids of Tshaka / Zulu *impis*, occurred between 1819 and 1832. Six Nguni-speaking groups savagely passed through the Rozvi kingdom during the *mfecane*, with the female warrior Nyamazana slaying Changamire Chirisamhuru at his court in 1831. (Zulu)

Mosi-wa-Tunya -------- rechristened the Victoria Falls by David Livingstone. One of the Seven Wonders of the World. (Tonga)

Muchongoyo ----------- An synchronised celebratory choreography. (Ndau)

Mutangakugara -------- Primordial Beginner; the Rozvi god present at the beginning.

Mwari -------------------- The Rozvi high god whose shrine was at Mtonjeni in the Matoba Hills in present day Matebeleland in Zimbabwe. The shrine was a cave from which the voice of the god allegedly spoke its oracles, often exhorting people to adhere to ancestral traditions.

N'anga ------------------- A traditional mediumistic doctor who divines to find the cause of illness and familial misfortunes, and prescribes

herbs for treatment. He is inferior to a territorial medium that he consults when faced with difficulties.
The name is derogatory if used on a supposed territorial medium. Unlike a *n'anga*, a territorial medium is mainly concerned with weighty territorial and kingly matters, and operates without herbs. (Rozvi)

Nduna ------------------- A Zulu/Ndebele counsellor or military commander.

Njuzu -------------------- A feared river goddess with the alleged anatomy of a mermaid.

Tumbare ---------------- Title for a Rozvi military leader who acted as curator or governor following the death or abduction of a king.